ROCK MUSIC SCENES IN BEIJING,
SHANGHAI & BEYOND

Andrew David Field

Rocking China

By Andrew David Field

ISBN-13: 978-988-8769-93-3

© 2023 Andrew David Field

MUSIC / Genres & Styles

EB181

All rights reserved. No part of this book may be reproduced in material form, by any means, whether graphic, electronic, mechanical or other, including photocopying or information storage, in whole or in part. May not be used to prepare other publications without written permission from the publisher except in the case of brief quotations embodied in critical articles or reviews. For information contact info@earnshawbooks.com

Published in Hong Kong by Earnshaw Books Ltd.

Prologue

In November 2006, I visited a rock music club in Beijing called Yugong Yishan 愚公移山, named after a famous Chinese proverb, "the stupid old man moves the mountain." This was one of several clubs and bars dedicated to a thriving rock music scene in the capital at the time. That evening, I witnessed two bands performing, the first a heavy metal band called Spring & Autumn (春秋) and the second an AC-DC cover band, both composed of Chinese and foreigners. In the small and gritty confines of the club, a mixed crowd also of Chinese and foreigners huddled around the stage as the bands played and sang their songs, creating a soundscape of raw energy that was translated into the kinetics of swaying and dancing bodies. I was deeply impressed with the two bands and the small yet lively and energetic scene I witnessed that evening. I returned to Beijing the following year and lived there for six months. Something exciting seemed to be going on with Beijing's rock scene, and I wanted to find out more.

During the summer and fall of 2007, I learned that the rock music scenes of Beijing, Shanghai, and other Chinese cities were breaking out of the 'underground' confines of small, sweaty clubs like Yugong Yishan. The club scenes provided the vital spark for these rock music scenes to thrive and flourish, but they weren't the only places where rock bands in China could be seen and heard. Music festivals also provided opportunities for rock bands to perform to much larger audiences. Chinese and international media were following the rock scenes in China and reporting about them to a wider public. And rock musicians and bands could share information about themselves as well as recordings of their music to a larger fan base via the internet. With hundreds of Chinese rock bands competing for attention on the stages of clubs and festivals, both in China and abroad, rock music was flourishing in China as never before.

Even so, the scene that I was following was still largely hidden and removed from the mainstream of Chinese popular culture and society. Because of its anti-conformist stance and its connections to youth protest culture, which had culminated in the protest movement of 1989, and for many other reasons, rock music had never been a widely accepted yet was a cherished grassroots form of popular culture in China as in the western world and in neighboring Japan and other Asian countries.

That situation would change over the next fifteen years, as some of China's indie rock bands went on to find a global audience and as the indie rock music scene in China generated even more domestic and international attention. Eventually, Chinese rock bands would gain a place in the online media sphere, where they attracted far larger audiences of Chinese youths than ever before. Until that time, the only Chinese rock bands that most people knew of, if any at all, were Cui Jian—the "godfather" of rock in China—and a few bands from the 1990s such as Tang Dynasty and Black Panther 黑豹. Nowadays, people who know something about rock music in China are also familiar with bands like Joyside, PK-14, Carsick Cars, SUBS, and Hedgehog—bands that I documented and interviewed in 2007 when they were still relatively unknown outside of China's urban rock music scene.

During the summer and fall of 2007 when I began this project, I witnessed, photographed, met, hung out with, and filmed dozens of bands performing in rock clubs and in music festivals in Beijing, Shanghai, and other cities in China. I also had extended conversations and conducted lengthy filmed interviews with rock musicians, band managers, club owners, record label founders, festival organizers, fans, and many others involved in the making of Chinese rock and roll. In the years that followed, I kept up with some of the scenes, the bands, and the folks whom I had met while embarking on this rock and roll journey.

Moving to Shanghai in 2008, where I have been based ever since, I co-produced an independent 'underground' documentary film on China's indie rock scene in 2012 called *Down: Indie Rock in the P.R.C.* Since then, we have screened this film at film festivals, academic conferences, universities, and other events all over the world. The film always generates many questions about the Chinese rock music scene, where it is going, and how it has developed since I filmed it in 2007.

Over the past fifteen years, I have kept up with the music scenes in China and revisited clubs and re-interviewed some of the key players in China's rock scenes from time to time. I eventually decided to pull together my experiences, documentations, and observations of the Chinese rock scene and write this book. My research materials consisted of 'field notes' I made through dozens of blogs that I posted on my website (shanghaisojourns. net) and dozens of hours of video that I shot of various club and festival scenes, as well as over a dozen one- to two-hour long interviews with key players in the scenes. As I wrote this book, using my collection of research materials as well as tapping into online resources, I was able to reconstruct the scenes I witnessed in fine detail.

I cannot claim this book to be a comprehensive study of the full diversity of rock bands and the wide range of sounds in China. That would be an impossible task for any single person to accomplish. Nor is this book meant to be a purely academic study of urban China's rock music scenes. I cannot claim to have captured all the vicissitudes of a scene that is constantly changing, with bands, clubs, promoters, and festivals coming and going over the years. Instead, this book captures an intense and significant moment in the recent history of rock music in China, mainly taking place in the year 2007, and then follows some of the bands, clubs, and scenes that I then witnessed as they continued to develop over the next fifteen years or so. In this sense it is more along the lines of a journalistic record as well as a personal memoir of my experiences and observations while documenting the rock scenes in China. This book is based on extensive interviews I conducted with dozens of key people involved in the rock scenes of China, as well as firsthand observations from dozens of live music events in China that I attended over the past fifteen years. It is intended for readers who are interested in what has been going on in China over the past few decades as the country opened to influences from abroad, and how China has been integrating with, absorbing, and reshaping international cultural trends.

While writing this book I have taken inspiration from fine journalistic writing about Chinese society in recent decades. One prime example is the work of Peter Hessler, who I met in 2006 during the same visit to Beijing that first inspired this project. His meticulous notetaking, empathetic interviewing and descriptive writing style have inspired me to incorporate fine details that enhance and enrich the portrayals of people and scenes in China. I was also inspired by the work of Jonathan Campbell, whose book *Red Rock* still stands as the definitive account of the history of rock music in China. This is one of many publications by Earnshaw Books, and I could not imagine a better publisher for this book, which fills in some of the gaps between Campbell's broad history of rock in China and the developments of the past ten years or so, while at the same time diving deeper into the indie music scene of the 2000s.

Colleagues in my field of China studies who have both inspired and encouraged me to write about rock music in China include Andreas Steen, Andrew Jones, Jeroen de Kloet, and Jeroen Groenewegen. I owe a special debt of gratitude to James Farrer, with whom I co-wrote our book *Shanghai Nightscapes*, who taught me a great deal about interviewing, on-site observing, and writing over the years.

I should also take a moment to thank my filmmaking partner Jud Willmont for his steady encouragement and support over the years. And I need to thank Graham Earnshaw for his patience and guidance as I completed this book project, as well as many other projects on which we have collaborated over the years.

Above all, I wish to thank all the people who participated in my rock documentation project, especially Michael Pettis, owner of the groundbreaking club D-22, Yang Haisong, lead singer of PK-14, and Kang Mao and Wu Hao, the two core members of the band SUBS. In addition, the members of the bands Hedgehog, Lonely China Day, Guai Li, Joyside, PK-14, Brain Failure, Carsick Cars, Spring & Autumn, and many other rock bands based in Beijing were especially helpful and inspirational for this project. Interviews and discussions with Matthew Kagler, Ed Peto, Tamsin Roberts, Liu Miao and Gao Feng, and Lao Yang also helped to expand and deepen my understanding of the Beijing music scene.

Kaiser Kuo—a founding member of Tang Dynasty, later a member of Spring & Autumn, and now a well-known podcaster—also provided some initial guidance and direction during the early phase of my research.

I hope that this book captures some of the energy and spirit of the Beijing indie rock scene in its heyday in the 2000s, and that it illuminates the process by which rock music spread to other cities, places and spaces in China as the rock scene has become more localized, decentralized, and diversified over the past two decades. Moreover, I hope that it reveals the indomitable spirit of the Chinese people as they continue to struggle and search for new and innovative means of self-expression and to build deep and lasting connections with the wider world, while forging their own unique identities, aspirations, and experiences.

Introduction

ROCK MUSIC experienced a belated entry into China. During the Cultural Revolution era of 1966-76, the rock-and-roll revolution taking place elsewhere around the world had no effect on China, even though, as Andrew Jones argues in his book *Circuit Listening* (2020) there were interesting parallels between western rock songs and the short and punchy paeans to Chairman Mao that could be heard on every tinny loudspeaker across the Chinese nation. It is hard to imagine that until the 1980s, almost nobody living in China had ever heard of Elvis Presley or the Beatles — no wonder that the Beatles' song 'Revolution' criticized people who went around carrying pictures of Chairman Mao. Along with other forms of western-influenced popular music, rock music first entered China after the death of Mao in 1976. This happened during the dawn of the new era of 'reforms and opening' (*gaige kaifang*) launched in 1978 by China's next leader, Deng Xiaoping.

The early history of rock music in 1980s China was characterized by the epic search for new sounds and styles that incorporated some local or regional Chinese musical and cultural traditions into rock music imported from abroad. This happened largely in the capital city of Beijing through the pioneering contributions of musicians like China's 'rock godfather' (摇滚教父), Cui Jian, as well as Tang Dynasty, Black Panther, and other legendary Chinese rock bands and musicians from that era. Most of their musical influences came from the more 'mainstream' rock and pop bands of the western world, such as the Beatles, the Rolling Stones, Led Zeppelin, Rush, Bon Jovi, The Police,

ROCKING THE CHINESE NATION

Peter Gabriel, Guns 'N Roses, and many other bands that were dominating the airwaves in the USA, the UK and Europe.

The first big western pop band to perform in China in 1985 was Wham!, whose lead singer George Michael later went on to even greater fame as a solo artist. Performing in front of a crowd of thousands in the Beijing Workers' Stadium, this band proved influential to a whole generation of young Chinese including Cui Jian, who began his musical career as a trumpeter in a Beijing orchestra. Switching to guitar and backed by a band consisting of several Chinese and foreign musicians, including his partner Liu Yuan on saxophone and a Chinese instrument called *suona* 唢呐, Cui Jian went on in 1986 to launch his own bid for rock stardom. During a concert featuring other Chinese singers and musicians, he announced his new career to China by singing his soulful rock song 'I Have Nothing' (一无所有) in front of another enthusiastic crowd of thousands, also in the Beijing Workers' Stadium. Cui Jian's band and other early Chinese rock bands such as Tang Dynasty and Black Panther went on to make names for themselves in China and elsewhere in Asia as rock stars and recording artists.

This creative process of building up a body of *yaogun*, or Chinese rock music, happened in fits and starts. It was punctuated by the 1989 protest movement that culminated in the bloody crackdown of June 4. During the daring and ultimately tragic movement that unfolded that spring (which I watched on CNN while attending Dartmouth College after my first visit to China in the winter of 1989), Cui Jian and other rock musicians such as Beijinger He Yong and the songwriter from Taiwan, Hou Dejian, performed their music to enormous crowds of protestors at Tiananmen Square. Cui Jian's song 'I Have Nothing' became an anthem of the movement. In the aftermath of the crackdown, Cui Jian and many other rock musicians continued to perform live, but rock music was pushed 'underground' by a government that connected rock music with political protest culture. Perhaps the leaders of China had some inkling of the strong connections between rock music and politics that had helped bring down the Berlin Wall in 1989 and had helped to catalyze the collapse of the Soviet Union in 1991. Thus, the great rock and roll revolution in China was postponed for at least another decade.

It is important also to keep in mind that during this era, both western and Chinese rock music were absent from the mass media of radio, television, and film in China. By the mid-1990s, there were a few radio stations that dared to play some rock songs, but only in big cities, and they did so under the constant threat of having performances shut down by authorities. So how did budding rock musicians in China originally find their influences and learn their craft? Rock and pop music from the outside world first infiltrated into China in the 1980s, mainly through the novel technology of audio cassette tapes, which were endlessly copied and shared and played on tape players, which Chinese were beginning to purchase at that time. Most of the music coming into China then featured the 'sweet' pop music of singers from Taiwan—most notably Deng Lijun, also known as Teresa Teng, whose music was even broadcast across the Taiwan strait in the late 1970s to win the hearts and minds of the Chinese people. At the same time, rock music from the western world was also being introduced to Chinese ears by way of cassette tapes, particularly by foreign students who were studying in Chinese universities, but also by a new cadre of journalists, diplomats and businesspeople coming in from abroad. Some even brought their own instruments.

Graham Earnshaw was one of the journalists who first brought the sounds of rock and pop music from the West into China in the late 1970s and early 1980s. In 1979, Graham first arrived in

ROCKING THE CHINESE NATION

Beijing as a journalist and brought a guitar with him. He formed a band with some other western expats called The Peking All-Stars which performed regularly through to 1984. Graham Earnshaw said the band was one of the earliest influences on Cui Jian and other Chinese rockers from that pioneering age — performances at the Friendship Hotel were the first time these kids had ever experienced the power of four-on-the-floor rock, with drums and bass, lead guitar and a vocalist shouting into a microphone. In an interview with him in 2016, I asked Graham Earnshaw about his relationship with Cui Jian in those early days. He told me that Cui Jian and another young musician named Liu Yuan used to hang out in the places where his band was performing and rehearsed with the band on several occasions. Cui was a trumpeter and Liu was a sax player, both classically trained, and these two youths were eager to learn more about this energetic music coming from the western world. Eventually, Cui and Yuan would form their own band and start performing regularly in the 1980s, leading to Cui Jian's emergence as China's first big homegrown rock star later that decade. Graham Earnshaw's story is thus one of cultural

Graham Earnshaw plays rock and roll songs for a crowd of Chinese lao bai xing *(common folk) c. 1980. Source: Graham Earnshaw.*

transmission from a self-described 'mediocre' western musician (although Graham is an accomplished singer-songwriter) to two Chinese musicians who would become legendary figures in China's rock and jazz scenes over the next two decades.

Cui Jian was not the only Chinese rock star to come out of the tumultuous and experimental 1980s. Other bands were forming in the late 1980s as well. One of those was a now legendary rock band called Tang Dynasty (唐朝), whose story is well known. This band combined a 1980s heavy metal-influenced hard rock sensibility with Chinese lyrics that invoked a glorious past. The name of the band itself was indicative of the band's bid to connect progressive rock and roll music to a legendary 'golden age' in Chinese history. Another Beijing-based band that emerged during this era was Black Panther (黑豹), whose influences ranged from Bon Jovi to the Police and other popular rock bands from the West, yet who sang original songs in Chinese. The list goes on. By the late 1980s, Chinese rock music was beginning to come into its own, and long-haired rockers were performing their own styles of *yaogun*. Nevermore would Chinese people be content to hear amateur western expat bands perform covers of classic western rock and pop songs. They were hungry for their own bands, their own sounds, their own languages, and their own heroes of rock and roll.

Even so, it was exceedingly difficult for most people in China to gain access to rock music, whether produced by foreigners or by their own people. One way they did so was through the refuse produced by the western world and shipped to China in cargo containers. By the late 1990s, throwaway or 'cut' CDs, known in Chinese as *dakou* 打口, were streaming into China from the outside world in the millions, where they were sold on the black market for almost nothing. The arrival of these *dakou* CDs gave a new boost to the sheer variety of music accessible to Chinese listeners, although overall it was still fairly limited compared to what was being produced in the western world. Nevertheless, for Chinese musicians and music fans hungry for a much greater variety of music than was being offered in shops and on the radio, the *dakou* CDs were a godsend.

In 1996, when I first lived in Beijing for a six-month research stint as a graduate student, there were a few scattered clubs and bars in the city where people could listen to or play rock music. As I recall, the Chinese rock scene was very small, and it was still largely derivative. Most of these bands performed covers of popular or alternative rock bands from the USA or UK, including Nirvana, Oasis, the Cranberries, and Radiohead. The city of Shanghai, which I also lived in for two years during the late 1990s, was beginning to see the rise of live music clubs featuring mostly foreign musicians, who played a combination of jazz, blues, pop, and rock tunes. Even so, foreign and overseas Chinese musicians and music-lovers living in these cities proved influential in helping to spread the western culture of rock and roll into China, much as they had done for jazz music several decades earlier.

As David O'Dell narrates in his own memoir published in 2014, the Beijing punk scene was just beginning to emerge in the late 1990s. This scene grew out of student-oriented bars and clubs in Wudaokou near the campuses of China's top two universities, Peking University and Tsinghua University. As I also observed at the time, the scene was highly influenced by Nirvana and other 'grunge' bands from that era. By sharing mix tapes with Chinese rockers, David O'Dell and other visiting Americans also injected other sounds into the mix, including more progressive punk rock bands like the Bad Brains and Green Day. Other than circulating mix tapes brought into China from abroad by students and others, as mentioned above, Chinese youths had access to a greater variety of rock music and other styles of music through the phenomenon of the *dakou* CDs and the Wudaokou district of northwestern Beijing developed a vibrant black market for them. To be sure, they increased the scope and variety of rock bands and sounds that young Beijingers could access, but it was catch-as-catch-can when it came to these *dakou* CDs.

Whereas the 1980s saw the emergence of China's first rockers in the form of Cui Jian, Black Panther, Tang Dynasty, Cobra, and others, and the 1990s witnessed the birth of a punk movement in Beijing, the 2000s saw the dawn of a new era in which a far more diverse range of Chinese rock music competed for the attention of big city dwellers. This era witnessed the rise of what Chinese came to call *duli yaogun* (独立摇滚), or indie rock music. By the late 2000s, when I began to document the scene, there was a far greater number and variety of rock bands and musical styles in Beijing, Shanghai, and some other Chinese cities than I had seen a decade before.

This explosion of new sounds and styles was influenced and arguably brought about by the new media technology of the internet. With internet access spreading like wildfire in China since the early 2000s, coupled with the circulation of digitized music in the convenient and free form of the mp3 file, Chinese youths suddenly were able to gain access to pretty much the entire canon of western rock and pop music and therefore to a far greater variety of sounds, tastes, and styles, and genres of music than ever before. They also gained the ability to learn far more about both foreign and Chinese rock music through online media resources. Moreover, Chinese rock bands themselves were able to use the internet as a platform to promote their own music to a much wider audience.

At the same time, China's rapid globalization during the 2000s also contributed to the rise of this golden age of rock and roll. With China's entry into the World Trade Organization in 2001, and with major international events such as the 2008 Beijing Olympics and the 2010 Shanghai World Expo looming in the future, the 2000s saw a massive increase in the number and variety of foreigners and overseas Chinese who came to work, study, teach, invest, build businesses, and enjoy life in large Chinese cities. Chinese musicians living in these cities now had a much bigger audience for their live performances. They also had the opportunity to make direct contact with potentially hundreds of musicians, DJs, band managers, record producers, and music aficionados coming to China from abroad. These people brought with them new styles, instruments, technologies, and ways of performing and recording music. The growing numbers of foreign and overseas Chinese living in Beijing, Shanghai and elsewhere in China in the 2000s spurred on the rise of a much greater number of clubs dedicated to the performance of rock music, as well as other more niche forms of performance culture, such as jazz, blues, electronica, and hip-hop clubs. It was within this urban milieu that a new scene consisting of young Chinese musicians striving for creative new sounds and styles was born, and the indie rock revolution in China was launched.

By the 2000s, several dedicated rock clubs existed in Beijing, Shanghai, and a few other Chinese cities like Guangzhou down south, and Wuhan in central China. Even in late 1990s, in Wudaokou, one could visit the Scream Bar, whose owner Lu Bo started one of the first indie rock labels, Scream Records (Field 2018). This bar nurtured a nascent punk and post-punk rock music scene whose early contributors included the bands New Pants (新裤子), PK-14, and Cold-Blooded Animals (冷血动物) led by the wraithlike Xie Tianxiao.

Other rock clubs opened in the early 2000s. By the mid-2000s, the city saw the emergence of a more sophisticated live music scene consisting of several clubs, including Yugong Yishan, Dos Kolegas, and D-22. When I arrived in Beijing in 2007 to document the city's rock music scene, another club called MAO Livehouse had just been added to the roster. In addition, there was a larger venue called Star Livehouse, where more famous players could perform. Shanghai also had a few live bars catering to the growing indie music scene in that city, though most of the bands were brought down to Shanghai from Beijing. At that time, on the eve of the 2008 Beijing Olympics, China's capital city was the undisputed center of rock music in China and would remain so for a few more years to come. Little did I know at the time that I would witness and document a golden age in the development of indie rock music in Beijing and in China.

1
MAPPING THE ROCK CLUB SCENES OF BEIJING

IN THE 1980s, Beijing was the birthplace of *yaogun* in China. By the 2000s, Beijing was unquestionably the most important city in China for the rise of a new era of Chinese rock and roll. The nation's capital attracted thousands of ambitious musicians and artists from all over China and the world. While some played on the bigger stages and in the larger arenas of the city, most became part of the 'underground' scene of small, gritty rock clubs that could be found in various neighborhoods throughout the city (see Map 1). In fact, there were only a few clubs that were truly pushing the envelope in terms of providing a space for rock musicians to experiment, invent, and produce their own original sounds. These clubs included Yugong Yishan, 2 Kolegas, 13 Club, D-22, and MAO Live House. Each of these clubs produced its own specific scene, which favored certain kinds and styles of rock music and bands and attracted fans of those types of music. Nevertheless, there was considerable overlap among these club scenes in terms of the bands, fans, and styles of music they represented, and all of them could be said to be vigorous promoters of original Chinese rock music.

One key ingredient that all these clubs shared was the close affinity of the bands to the audience. During the performances and between them, musicians and their fans mixed, mingled, drank, and danced together in these clubs as they indulged their

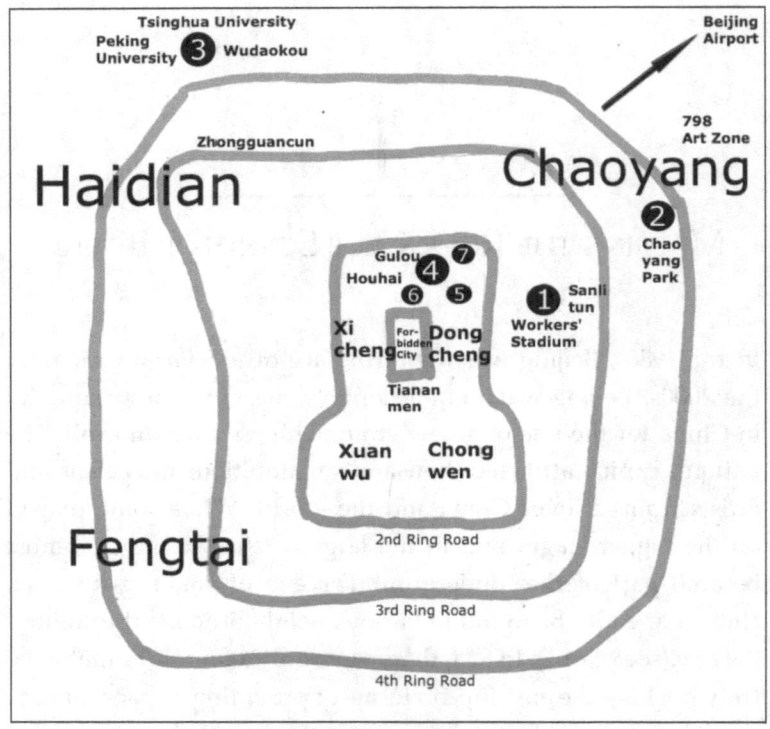

Map 1: Rock Clubs in Beijing, 1990s-2010s

(1) Old Yugong Yishan (2004-2006); (2) 2 Kolegas; (3) 13 Club and D-22; (4) MAO Live House; Temple Bar; (5) New Yugong Yishan (2007-); (6) XP; (7) School Bar

appetites for original and inventive rock music. The intimacy between the bands and their fans was extremely important for the transmission of indie rock in China, since theoretically anybody could take up the guitar, grab a mic, and sing their own original songs if they were so inspired. While most of the people attending these clubs remained fans, the clubs served as important incubators for budding musicians from all over China to learn more about the art of rock and roll, to engage directly with other musicians, and to experiment with, refine, develop, and stretch their own musical and performance styles.

ANDREW DAVID FIELD

My own introduction to Beijing's rock scene came in 2006 with a fortuitous visit to a club called Yugong Yishan, or 'The Stupid Old Man Moves the Mountain' in English. The name is from a famous Chinese proverb about an old man who with great stubbornness and perseverance was able to move an entire mountain that blocked his view — or at least, his stubbornness convinced a deity to do the job for him. This was a favorite slogan of Chairman Mao and it played a role in the politics of the Cultural Revolution of 1966-1976, when the entire country entered a tumultuous era of political violence as the youths of China, emboldened by Mao, set out to smash the remnants of old feudal or imperial culture.

Now, thirty years after the end of the Cultural Revolution, China was going through another era of violent transformation as the infusion of capital and culture from abroad was leading to the destruction of old neighborhoods and ways of life, and the creation of new ones. This was the beginning of a period of rampant gentrification in large cities like Beijing and Shanghai. When I visited Yugong Yishan at around 10 p.m. on the cold autumn night of 24 November 2006, the venue was already slated for imminent demolition in an unstable urban landscape that was constantly being reshaped by developers.

The club was located across from the Worker's Stadium in eastern Beijing. Its main hall was small, cozy, and warm, with walls painted a murky shade of red, and already it was filling up with patrons. On the elevated stage, lit up by multi-colored spotlights and close enough for us to reach out and touch them or at least see the sweat dripping down their foreheads were five sturdy men playing up a storm. Four of them had long flowing hair, typical of metal rockers in China and abroad. Only the drummer wore his hair shortly cropped. This was the Beijing metal band known as Chun Qiu 春秋 or 'Spring & Autumn'.

Fronting the band was lead singer, songwriter, and guitarist

ROCKING THE CHINESE NATION

Yang Meng, a lean and wiry fellow who hailed from Yunnan Province in southwest China. On guitars were two larger men, Kou Zhengyu and Kaiser Kuo, both giants in the Chinese metal scene. They exchanged leads, harmonizing and soloing gracefully as the band played on, filling the Beijing night with the powerful sound of metal guitar music. Obviously, they had been playing together for many years. Keeping rhythm were Li Bo on the electric bass and Diao Lei pounding the drums at the back of the stage and smiling at his bandmates as if they were all in on a secret joke.

Inside the small standing-room-only club was a crowd of rock enthusiasts. The crowd waxed and waned over the evening, as some people headed out to other more disco-oriented clubs surrounding the Workers' Stadium or into the nearby bar and club district known as Sanlitun, arguably the liveliest neighborhood in town catering to an international crowd of night owls. Others washed into the club from nearby restaurants and bars, beers

Spring & Autumn (春秋) play at the old Yugong Yishan on 24 Nov. 2006 (photo by Andrew Field)

in hand. At first the audience was mainly Chinese, although it included a fair share of foreigners. Most people looked to be in their 20s or 30s. While some hung out at the bar in the back of the club, most were standing closer to the stage, watching the act on stage with great enthusiasm and intensity.

The band played a series of original tunes from their eponymous CD album *Spring and Autumn*, which I purchased in the club at the end of their concert. The songs they played that night included 'Spring Water Flows East' (春水向东流), a melodic and contemplative tune reminiscent of a more traditional Chinese folk song. That song was followed by the more metallic song 'Legend' (传奇). Like 'Spring Water,' 'Legend' also started out in a somewhat folksy style and then it quickly morphed into a high-energy, head-banging series of harmonized guitar riffs. Later in the song, the guitarists swapped a set of solos. 'What are we?' shouted Yang Meng in Chinese, and then he answered his own question: 'We are ourselves/We're making legends within the contradiction.'

What is the 'contradiction' in question? Is it the painfully obvious one between China's frenzied market-oriented modernization drive with its collective desire to be more international, more Western, more open, and particularly more American, versus the Communist Party leadership still holding onto its vision of central control for the Chinese nation? Or is it the contradiction between a hurried urban life full of influences and promises from the outside world, versus the hardscrabble existence in bucolic rural villages and small towns that most Chinese over the millennia have experienced until recently? Nobody but Yang Meng knew the answer to this question, and perhaps even he himself would be hard pressed to say.

Next up was their song 'A Call from Afar' (远方的召唤), which also had both a folksy sound and an edgy rawness to it. In the song, Yang Meng called out for his 'slaves' to come sing and dance with him, to move their bodies to the rhythm of the song. Anybody familiar with the legendary Chinese rocker Cui Jian might catch the reference to his early hit, 'Nothing to My Name,' which he and his band debuted to the Chinese people during a now legendary concert held at the Workers' Stadium across the road in 1986. Yet instead of phrasing it as a question, it came in the form of a demand: Not 'When will you go with me?' as Cui Jian pleaded to his audience, but rather the commanding, 'Come with me now, my slaves!'

The mixture of fast-paced metal guitar riffs with Chinese lyrics and folk elements blended well and gave the band's music an epic quality. This was music made for the nomads of China, those restless masses looking for better lives in the big cities. Yang Meng sang his own lyrics in clear and audible tones, inviting his Chinese listeners to embark on a journey into the fictive imagination of this Yunnanese songwriter. Influenced by Buddhism and Daoism, his songs evoked powerful nature images of mountains, rivers, thunder, and rain. The song 'Between the Mountains and the Sea' (山海间) was replete with Daoist imagery. It started out beautifully with Yang Meng plucking out a tune on his guitar with elegant slides that make it sound like a Chinese zither. One could envision a man wandering alone on a journey, a tiny figure in a sea of mountains and clouds, as in a Chinese landscape painting. The song is contemplative and philosophical, invoking the void, the emptiness of space, which many of the great landscape paintings in Chinese art history capture.

That night, to the thunderous drums and the sounds of electric guitars, Yang Meng was chanting out a beautiful and serene Chinese landscape through music. He was one left behind by hundreds of millions of rural-urban migrants who, like the singer himself, had made their way from the vast interior of China to the big coastal cities to make a living. China was and still is in the greatest phase of human migration in world history. Maybe the figure of 'A Call from Afar' is the capitalist master, the factory owner urging his 'slaves' from the impoverished countryside to come and toil in his dark satanic mills. Or maybe the master in question is the government of China, and this is in fact a political protest song.

Or could we just be over-interpreting a song that is simply meant to be fun—and perhaps it was just playful Yang Meng himself 'enslaving' his audience by making them sing and dance to his own tunes? Then again, this being metal rock, maybe Satan was the enslaver in question. Regardless of the meaning or intent of the lyrics, the largely Chinese audience danced and headbanged on, possibly oblivious to the meaning and import of the lyrics. Ultimately it was the energy and spirit of the performance, along with the adrenalin and heat that the band was generating on a cold Beijing night in November, that really mattered.

Spring & Autumn finished their gig by around 11 p.m., and the sweaty band members hustled off the stage to let another band take the spotlight. The second band called themselves Dirty Deeds after one of the songs by the famed hard rock band AC/DC. The lead singer, an American and long-term Beijing resident named Jaime Welton, had a long, curly hairdo and sported the cocky, badass attitude of a '70s rocker. Kaiser Kuo remained on stage and took on the role of AC/DC's guitarist Malcolm Young. A white male guitarist with short-cropped black hair took the part of Malcolm's brother Angus, wearing only a signature pair of schoolboy shorts and no shirt. Jaime Welton played the role of Bon Scott or his posthumous replacement Brian Johnson, matching the visceral energy, the taunting, and the high-pitched screaming of AC/DC's lead singer, as the tribute band performed a series of their most famous tunes, including 'Rosy' and 'TNT' among others. During the song 'TNT,' the band urged the crowd to join them in the chorus of OI's that start the song, raising their fists in unison. Again, Jaime exhorted the crowd to join him in the chorus of 'TNT', after pausing for effect: '…..cause I'm TNT'. The crowd obliged, almost in unison. They were now *his* slaves. By this time, the audience had changed over to mostly foreigners and the energy of the room reached its peak, with dozens of young men and women dancing wildly with booze- and adrenaline-fueled ecstasy as they interpret the familiar music with their bodies. The show ended well after the midnight hour, and everyone spilled out of the club heading home or to the next venue for some more nocturnal fun.

That night I bore witness to one of the final performances at the old club venue of Yugong Yishan. Soon afterwards, the club was demolished to make way for a shopping mall, and the club itself moved to another location in the city, where it would continue to serve as a venue for a wide variety of musical styles and genres encapsulated within the larger framework of 'indie

Two good buddies: Gao Feng (l) and Liu Miao (r), co-owners of the club 2 Kolegas, during an interview with the author (video still by Andrew Field)

rock.' To be sure, Spring & Autumn was a metal band, and as such, they differentiated themselves from the indie rock scene and identified themselves as being part of the Chinese metal scene. Nevertheless, all these bands were producing their own original music and releasing it independently of the western-dominated pop music industry, and in that sense, these were all indie rock bands.

The Eclectic, Grungy Scene at 2 Kolegas in the Chaoyang Park district

Another scene-making club in Beijing was Dos (or 2) Kolegas. Known in Chinese as 'two good buddies' (两个好朋友), the club was named after the pair of musicians who founded it. The club was in the eastern Chaoyang district, which with its embassies, international offices and hotels boasts the highest concentration of foreigners in the city. My own observations through numerous site visits to the club since 2007 as well as testimony from the club managers suggests that most people attending this club were foreigners, although it did attract a fair number of Chinese customers as well, especially rock musicians and other scene-makers. The club was off Liangmaqiao Road, between the Third Ring Road and Fourth Ring Road, skirting the northern edge of Chaoyang Park. While somewhat distant from the famed nightlife neighborhood of Sanlitun, it was in a district with plenty of late-night bars and clubs that cater to a Chinese and foreign nightclubbing crowd, such as The World of Suzie Wong located on the eastern edge of Chaoyang Park. Yet because of its out-of-the-way location north of the park, 2 Kolegas did not attract a great deal of spillover from these other bars and clubs. Instead, most of its patrons were avid rock music enthusiasts, who knew something about the Chinese rock scene or at least were curious about it.

ROCKING THE CHINESE NATION

To get to 2 Kolegas from Liangmaqiao Road, one entered a driveway leading to an open-air drive-in cinema and then around a bend to the club itself. Situated amongst a row of other small clubs and bars, 2 Kolegas was built into a long, single story and rather makeshift building. Its outer and inner walls were all covered in colorful graffiti. Fronting the club was a large grassy yard, though the grass had been worn down with the heels of people walking around outside the club. Surrounding the building was a forest of poplar trees, making it an ideal spot for late-night music played at high volume. Despite being a small and relatively out-of-the-way club in eastern Beijing, 2 Kolegas boasted one of the most eclectic music scenes in the city.

Liu Miao and Gao Feng, the two owners and managers of 2 Kolegas, were both musicians. At the time I frequented the club in 2007, Liu Miao played drums for a band called Nuclear. While Liu Miao had long rocker hair and wore glasses, Gao Feng cultivated a wispy beard and mustache, and his hair was shaved short. Both men are stocky and sturdy fellows. During my interview with them, Liu Miao was the bigger talker, while Gao Feng was more reserved. Together they explained that along with one other employee, they managed everything from booking bands to getting posters and gig promotions in the local media to stocking and serving alcohol to manning the stage and sound controls. This helped to explain why the club had some difficulties with managing the sound quality along with the myriad other affairs of the bar and the bands.

Despite these challenges, the club managed to attract many different types of rock bands and a wide variety of fans. Most of the shows that I attended at 2 Kolegas in 2007 and in subsequent years attracted a mixed crowd of curious foreigners of all ages, as well as youthful Chinese rock fans. During the interview, Gao Feng remarked, 'Most of them are coming for the music.

They like music, and they especially like live music. Lots of our customers are musicians themselves. It's easy for us all to make friends, since because of our love for playing music, we all have a lot to talk about.' When I asked them what sort of contribution their club is making to the rock scenes of Beijing, his partner Liu Miao answered: 'Our contribution is that we enable more bands, especially bands that have already made names for themselves, to have more opportunities to perform, and we bring their music to a wider audience. Also, we provide a space for all those people who love to get together and play in this kind of scene.' Gao Feng interjected: 'How to say it—every club is different, totally different.'

'Yes, the atmosphere is different, the feeling is different,' Liu Miao continued. 'Like if you go to MAO Live House, as soon as you enter, you feel that it's different. If you go to D-22, completely different. Every club has its differences.'

While the two musicians didn't articulate these differences any further, the overall message was clear: Each club in the city developed its own special scene out of the combination of 'atmosphere'—including the design of the space, the décor, and the clientele—as well as the 'feeling' it generated, and of course, through the specific bands and styles of musicians each club attracted.

CH+INDIE Fest at 2 Kolegas (8-9 July 2007)

In the summer of 2007, the city was gearing up for its big international debut as the host of the Summer Olympic Games in 2008. As a local news article reported, 67,000 taxis were busy being de-odorized and their drivers were all taking crash courses in English. Many of the ancient *hutong* neighborhoods consisting of labyrinths of alleyways full of courtyard houses dating back to the Ming dynasty that were once the very warp and woof of

Beijing society, were being knocked down or else prettified and commercialized. Old streets were being repaved, old buildings painted over, and odd-looking new buildings were rising by the dozens, including the CCTV Headquarters building designed by the architect Rem Koolhaas, known locally as 'The Pants'. The Olympic stadium designed by famed artist Ai Weiwei, known to everyone as the 'Bird's Nest', was also well under construction, as was the rest of the apparatus for the Olympic Games.

On a hot, wet July afternoon, I hailed a cab from Beijing Capital Normal University where I was staying in the western Haidian district and took it across the city via the ring roads from west to east. The taxi passed endless boxy buildings, many of them built in the previous ten years or so, and many others still under construction with cranes beside them. Finally, after nearly one hour in heavy Beijing traffic, my taxi arrived at 2 Kolegas. That weekend, the club was hosting a special event dubbed the CH+INDIE Fest. Since this was the second year of the festival, they decided to name it 'CH+INDIE Fest II: The Wrath of Khan', alluding to the original Star Trek film series.

On the first day of the concert, I watched a flashy punk band from Xi'an called No Name perform on the outdoor stage. They were decked out in outfits of black leather, their hair punked out and their bodies covered with tattoos, as they performed a set of angry songs. As if carried away by their music, a sudden gust of wind bearing a rainstorm suddenly ripped the event banner behind the stage, causing it to flap about in the wind and forcing the band off the stage, as people scrambled to save the equipment from the rainstorm and carry it inside. Given the rainy day, it was little wonder that the audience on the first day was much smaller than the expected crowd of several hundred the organizers had planned for. While the intention of the festival organizers was to hold the festival outdoors, the rain forced the bands inside to perform onstage in the tiny club, which was much too small and crowded a space for the size of audience the organizers intended to attract. Later that evening, Liu Miao's band Nuclear performed with the club's co-owner on drums, as his partner Gao Feng ran around the club trying to manage the sound system as well as the bar. The final event of the evening was a punk band called Brain Failure (I will return to this band later in the book).

I returned to the club the following day. It had stopped raining, but just in case, the performances were still being held inside the club. When I met Matt Kagler on the afternoon of the second day of the festival, he was at a booth outside the club selling entrance tickets. With his purple-and-red plaid collared shirt, black-framed glasses, and imposing red beard, he stood out from the rest of the indie crowd. The red beard and shirt suggested to me that he'd be equally comfortable sporting a tartan and blowing on a set of bagpipes as standing in front of

Matt Kagler, owner of Tag Team Records at CH+INDIE Fest at 2 Kolegas, 9 July 2007 (photo by Andrew Field)

a Beijing club hawking tickets for an indie rock festival. Then again, his impressive physical girth, plaid shirt, hefty beard, and glasses also gave him the look of a hipster lumberjack.

I asked Matt to say a few words on camera about the festival. He replied in a slightly blasé tone: 'It's basically a showcase of local Beijing bands that are pretty much the upper echelon of local Beijing bands *per se*—at least we think so, and most of the press think so.' The bands at the festival included punk/post-punk bands Brain Failure (the headliner of the first night), Arrows Made of Desire, Dead J, Hedgehog, Joyside, Lonely China Day, Nuclear, Snapline, Sound Fragment, SUBS, Sulumi, Casino Demon, Scoff, and No Name. Aside from Arrows Made of Desire, a band on the Tag Team record label fronted by a Swedish guitarist/singer named Mikael, all the others were Chinese bands based in Beijing.

Matt was the owner of Tag Team Records, an indie record label based in Beijing. He co-organized the event along with Modern Sky, one of the leading indie record labels in the city. I asked him which bands he believed were the best in the festival.

'In my opinion,' he replied, 'probably Lonely China Day and Hedgehog are my favorite bands that are playing today, but I like all of them, or I wouldn't have booked them. SUBS are gonna headline, and they're a big draw—they're more sort of like, post-punk, punk sort of thing, and we like that as well, I mean, all of it's really high-quality stuff.'

The four band members of SUBS were sitting around a table outside on the grassy lawn, rapping with Jaime Welton, the singer for the local AC/DC-cover band Dirty Deeds. Jaime was sporting a pair of camo shorts and a black sleeveless t-shirt with a white crab on the chest, which gave full display to an awesome Chinese dragon tattooed on his right arm and shoulder. He was deep in conversation in Chinese with SUBS bassist Zhu Lei, who also had long, dark and tousled hair, and wore a black t-shirt blazoned with the name of punk band Last Call Brawl from Long Island, New York. Sitting on his other side was the lead guitarist Wu Hao, aka Kosmo Wu, wearing a white tank top and dark jeans. His hair was grown out not quite to shoulder length. On his neck, a five-pointed red star hung from a necklace, and on the middle finger of his left hand was a large black polished gemstone. He had a boyish and somewhat puffy face. Next to him sat drummer Zhang Shun, with his hair hanging down Emo style in front of his eyes, wearing a white SUBS t-shirt, and looking gaunt and haggard and slightly hung over. Beside him was SUBS lead singer, Kang Mao. Her hair was shorter than the rest of her bandmates, and she had a pair of white-rimmed sunglasses and large, white-hooped earrings to match. She seemed to be bursting with energy. Her eyes darted around curiously as she took in the conversations around her. She was also wearing a black tank top, revealing on her left shoulder her own signature tattoo: a cute, furry, large-eyed black cat.

Surrounding the SUBS band members were several other tables with around thirty people sitting under their own umbrellas and drinking water or sipping beers. Most were foreigners. A tall, thin British DJ named Ian Sherman was choosing and changing CDs on a Pioneer console and blasting music to the outdoor crowd. Most of these songs were 'retro' tunes from the 1960s. While I was interviewing Matt Kagler, we could hear the 1966 garage rock song '96 Tears' by Question Mark and the Mysterians. Ian Sherman had on a turquoise t-shirt. With his reddish hair, aquiline nose, and pointy Van Dyke beard, he looked a bit like Charles I of England as rendered by the beard's namesake. It turned out that Ian was the 'first mate' of Tag Team Records, and he also wrote pieces about the city's indie music scene and published them online.

ROCKING THE CHINESE NATION

Beijing punk band Joyside performing at 2 Kolegas during the CH+INDIE Fest on 9 July 2007

While Ian Sherman was playing music to the outdoor crowd, we could hear the band inside warming up and going through their sound check. I observed and filmed several bands over the two-day festival. The standouts in my opinion were three bands who played consecutively on the second night of the festival and who reflected the eclecticism of the 2 Kolegas club scene: Joyside, Lonely China Day, and SUBS.

Joyside

Later in the day, I headed into the club to catch the band Joyside, one of the favored bands of the punk scene in Beijing. As of 2007, they had already been featured in at least two documentary films focusing on Chinese punk rockers: *Wasted Orient* (dir. Kevin Fritz, 2006) and *Beijing Bubbles* (dir. George Lindt, 2005). The tall and slender lead singer, Bian Yuan, also known by his English name of Billy, had a moppish hairdo and his long hair partly shielded his eyes. Next to him on stage was a husky bassist named Liu Hao, who sported a black shirt with pink polka dots.

On his other side was guitarist Liu Hongwei. Backing them was drummer Guan Zheng.

Their music was primal and rhythmic, with Bian Yuan chanting and sometimes screaming out the lyrics in a scratchy voice, the product of many cigarettes and beers. Some of their tunes had a Ramones-like quality to them. Others were reminiscent of Sex Pistols or Iggy Pop. The titles of their albums *Drunk is Beautiful* (2004) and *Bitches of Rock'n'Roll* (2006) give one a sense of what their music is about, as do the song titles, such as 'I Want Beer,' 'Music Sucks,' 'I Wanna Piss Around You', 'Hey Bitch!', and 'Eat Me'. Billy handled the verses, and the whole band joined in for the chorus.

The crowd by now was completely lost in the music, dancing around the room, with a whirlpool of wicked energy gathering near the stage. A young German man with a pointy Mohawk that greatly accentuated his modest stature was busy swirling

The three band members of indie rock band Hedgehog (far right and foreground) slam dance with other audience members to the songs of Joyside at the CH+INDIE Fest at 2 Kolegas in July 2007. Behind them, smoking a cigarette and sporting a fedora is Leo from The Scoff (photo by Andrew Field)

his arms and legs about in a delicate choreography, aiming to bump and nudge but not bash the others in the mosh pit that had formed near the stage. The three members of another young band called Hedgehog (whom I describe later in this book), who had just finished a performance of their own music, were caught up in the mix, their bodies drenched in sweat, with huge ecstatic grins on their faces. The female drummer Atom, wearing a pink and purple striped shirt, was right there in the middle, her body whirling and twirling as she bumped up against her bandmates Zi Jian and Bo Xuan. Another Asian girl of about the same tiny size as Atom joined her in the fray. Everyone near the stage was lost in some ecstatic frenzy as they responded to the high energy of the band and the rebellious spirit of their music. Other musicians in the crowd, such as Leo, lead singer of the Beijing punk band Scoff, and the members of other bands mix in with the crowd, reflecting the intimate atmosphere of this club built around the tight camaraderie between the musicians and their fans.

Lonely China Day

Soon the sweaty beer-hall chants of Billy Bian and Joyside subsided to make way for the next band on the roster. This was Lonely China Day, the marquee band for Matt Kagler's indie record label Tag Team Records. By this time in the evening, the audience size was beginning to swell to well over one hundred people mashed together inside the brick-walled oven, awaiting the start of the band. As soon as they started, it was obvious that we were in for a completely different experience than what had come before.

Lit up by bars of pixelated light cast onto the wall behind them in a scene reminiscent of a cyberpunk novel, the two guitarists on stage appeared as if they themselves were broken into tiny

Wang Dongtao (l) and Deng Pei (r) of Lonely China Day perform at CH+INDIE Fest at 2 Kolegas on 9 July 2007 (photos by Andrew Field)

pixels of light. Deng Pei, the vocalist and songwriter of the band, was tall and wiry, with a powerful singing voice that ranged impressively in its highs and lows. He also had great stamina and in one breath he could handle a long vocal modulation up and down the scale, which was pentatonic. Unlike most of the punk bands who took the stage, who tended to sing in English, his lyrics were all sung in Chinese. Reading them in the Lonely China Day album liner notes requires knowledge of Classical Chinese, as they are influenced by the poetry of Tang and Song dynasties.

Deng Pei wore a red t-shirt and had short, tidy hair and slight sideburns. Dangling from his earlobe was a gold-hooped earring, and around his neck was a large pair of headphones. He used two microphones, one of which was nestled close to a megaphone taped onto a stand, which amplified his voice further as he sang his dirge-like chant amidst the arpeggios of his partner's guitar. In a pairing that called to mind John Lennon and Paul McCartney, he played his guitar left-handed, and so his actions mirrored those of his partner, Wang Dongtao, who was larger and more sturdily built than Deng Pei. Wang Dongtao was wearing a simple collared t-shirt zipped down to his chest. His hair was cut military-short and he had a big grin on his face as he played, with eyes that seemed to be looking on dreamily into another world. On his head, a pair of headphones covered his ears. His guitar work was steady, controlled, and methodical, consisting of arpeggiations that echoed in the room. Behind them, drummer Luo Hao kept a steady beat in 5-4 time.

They were performing their song 'Beijing Realize' which started out with a droning electronic sound that modulated into the lower registers and back up again. There was a 1960s feel to the song, with its radical experimentation with sonic textures, laid upon a simple melody on a blues base. One could hear echoes

The mixed audience of Chinese and foreigners, some obviously indie rock enthusiasts and insiders and others curious onlookers, watching the band Lonely China Day performing at CH+INDIE Fest at 2 Kolegas in July 2007. In the foreground is Meng Jinghui, manager of Hedgehog and some other bands in the scene (photo by Andrew Field)

of the Beatles' song 'Rain' in the electronic track which seemed to run backwards. When one heard the song, the words 'mantra' and 'trance' came immediately to mind. So did 'oceanic.'

One key to the band's composition lay in the lyrics themselves, which are hard to translate into English. Take the song 'Beijing Realize.' The song is a paean to the imperial capital of China, which Deng Pei claims to be 'in love with itself.' He sings of 'history's secrets' and of the 'pitiful days' of times past. There seems to be a self-referential, even self-parodying tone to the lyrics, with its references to the ancient imperial capital — and now the rock capital — of China. Deng Pei may be criticizing the vanity of a city that makes a pretense to being 'traditional' when it is in fact on a raging path towards the destruction of all traditions and has been for over half a century. Or maybe it is the vanity of the youths in the audience that he is targeting. He sings of 'puppets'. Who are they? Might they be the people of China?

Kang Mao (l) and Wu Hao (r) of SUBS performing at CH+INDIE Fest at 2 Kolegas on 9 July 2007. Behind Kang Mao is the bassist, Zhu Lei (photos by Andrew Field)

Or perhaps the officials themselves? Who knows? There may even be a reference here to Chairman Mao—might the 'pitiful days' remembered by old folks be the Cultural Revolution? Maybe there's even a veiled reference to the unmentionable events of 1989, which Deng Pei and others of his age may vaguely remember from their childhood—the misspent capital of youth 'blown at the emperor's feet.' Perhaps, then, the emperor mentioned in the song is another Deng, who led the country in its current direction of economic prosperity without making concessions to political reform. Aside from a few diehard fans, most of these lyrics were lost on the foreigner crowd mesmerized with the rhythmic power of the music itself.

SUBS

SUBS, the headlining act of the night, began their performance with a sonic boom. Wu Hao was strumming violently on his guitar as singer Kang Mao screamed out her song. At first, I found the sheer noisiness of the band off-putting after such a long two-day stretch of musical mayhem, and I headed outside for a break and a beer. A friend pulled me back into the club, urging me to see this band, and within a few minutes, I was completely smitten with the performance of Kang Mao. There was no holding back—she let out all her emotions on stage, screamed, gestured and jeered at the audience at the top of her lungs, cried and crooned, crawled on the floor, wrapped her mic cord around her neck to simulate a self-hanging, got down on the floor into what a yoga practitioner might recognize as the child's pose, then got up to rage and rant some more.

Throughout the 30-minute performance, Kang Mao was in constant motion as she strutted and fretted her way across the stage like a Shakespearean actress. Her band was tight and controlled, with Wu Hao and Zhu Lei backing her on vocals with their own refrains. Unlike some of the other bands whose performances were variable if not downright sloppy, they came across as extremely well-practiced, as if they had honed their game to a fine point. Their music was hard rock, yet deeply rooted in the blues. There were no fancy riffs or solos—just bone-shaking rhythmic rock music. While her sound was not in any way sweet or melodic, one could draw a legacy back to the great female blues singers of times past, from Bessie Smith to Janice Joplin and on to Kang Mao's own primal scream. The SUBS sound could also be compared to American hardcore bands like Fugazi, a band that Kang Mao herself referenced often when she talked about her own influences.

By this time of night, the audience was mainly foreigners, with a smattering of Chinese rockers thrown in the mix. The crowd was largely youthful, with some students from universities located on the west side of town, as well as plenty of white-collar workers and older folks from the east side. Inside the hot club near the stage, a few dozen people were dancing, with sweat running down their faces. There was a sexual vibe to the music, especially with Kang Mao fronting the band, with some couples grinding their bodies together to the music.

On that night and subsequently when I saw SUBS perform, it always seemed like a well-choreographed performance, which came across *in situ* as pure improvisation. After a few SUBS concerts, one caught the patterns in Kang Mao's own performances: the lying in the fetal position, the mic cord wrapped around the neck, and other bits that she integrated into her routine. Yet each performance seemed utterly genuine. She was an accomplished stage actress who played her role with great conviction, throwing her body and soul into it, no matter how large or small her audience may be. At one moment, she was a tormented woman, down on her knees, and at the next she was a raging torrent of anger, then she was begging somebody for forgiveness. Clearly, there was a heavy load of pent-up aggression in her act, and a great deal of personal sorrow and pain, which, as described later in the book, I found out more about while interviewing her and accompanying her and her band to their hometown of Wuhan.

The Student-Oriented Club Scene of Wudaokou

While 2 Kolegas was an important venue for indie rock bands to play to a small crowd of dedicated fans, it was in the western university district of Beijing that some of the most important incubators of Chinese indie rock music were located. Wudaokou is the name of a lively student-oriented neighborhood in the northwestern part of Beijing. It is located just to the east of the famed Summer Palace built by the 18th century Qing emperor Qianlong, with its large man-made lake and its Buddhist temples and arched bridges. Known for its high concentration of universities, the district also became known as the Silicon Valley of China, particularly around the nearby neighborhood of Zhongguancun, which became home to numerous start-up tech companies that spun out of the research centers of the universities nearby, including China University of Mining and Technology, Beijing Language and Culture University, and China University of Geosciences. A block or so north of those campuses is the Beijing Forestry University, and a block or so south of them are Beijing City University, Beijing University of Aeronautics, and University of Science and Technology Beijing. West of the intersection of Wudaokou and down the road a kilometer or so are China's two most famous and prestigious universities, Tsinghua University and Peking University. Given the large population of Korean students studying at the surrounding universities, this neighborhood also earned the nickname Koreatown, and indeed,

The exterior of club D-22 (video still image by Andrew Field)

the streets were chockablock with restaurants and bars catering to Korean students, who walked around in droves. There was also a sizeable population of international students from the Americas, Europe, and Africa. At night, the streets were alive with students noshing at dozens of outdoor food stalls and beer gardens or reeling from bar to bar. In the summer of 2007, the big nighttime lodestone of the neighborhood was an underground hip-hop club called Propaganda.

The Experimental Scene at D-22 in Wudaokou

Operating between 2006 and 2012, D-22 was a small rock club located on Chengfu Road just about a half kilometer west from the Wudaokou subway station, and even closer to the campuses of Tsinghua and Peking universities. Run by an American named Michael Pettis and managed by a Spanish American named Charles Saliba, the club attracted a mixed clientele of Chinese and foreigners. Many of those who attended concerts at D-22 were students from nearby universities, although it also attracted people from across the city as well, including many foreigners with an enthusiasm for the indie rock scene. The club space had a cozy, intimate feel to it, with the walls all painted red. One entered the club through an entrance foyer with a stall for selling entrance tickets as well as D-22 t-shirts, CDs of local rock bands, and other paraphernalia. Upon passing through the entranceway there was a bar on the left and a few tables and chairs laid out in the middle on a wooden floor. Beyond that was a smaller tiled floor where the audience could stand and watch the band on stage. The stage was only elevated a half-meter or so above the floor, and it was completely exposed on three sides, giving the bands maximum exposure to their audience.

Running alongside the stage to your left as you moved into the interior of the club was a narrow corridor lined with sofas where musicians lounged around chatting with their companions or waiting for their turn to perform. The bathrooms were in the back end, and they were in a word, gritty. As usual with clubs of this type, they were thickly festooned with graffiti. On the white walls of one of the bathrooms, a local Chinese artist had painted a startling set of images that blended into a grisly montage full

The artwork in the bathroom of D-22 in 2007 (photo by Andrew Field)

of skeletons, demon-like faces, angry punks spouting bubbles of nonsense in Chinese and English, towering, boiling Hiroshige-style waves, swirling vortices, insects, snakes coming out of people's mouths, fetal figures bubbling out of primordial ooze, and ubiquitous magic mushrooms.

On the white wall of another toilet chamber, running from ceiling to floor, there was a list of the names of local rock bands, regulars of the D-22 scene, written in capital letters with thick black markers:

Fire Balloon
Joyside
P.K.14
Hedgehog
Carsick Cars
Queensea Big Shark
Scoff
Hang on the Box
Demerit
Casino Demon
Gar
Guai Li
White
Arrows Made of Desire
RWF
No Name
Mold
Red Hand
Mafeisan
Snapline

These were all bands that had played at D-22 and for whom the club had helped establish their reputation in the Chinese indie rock scene. With the notable exception of Arrows Made of Desire, all these bands were composed mainly if not entirely of Chinese musicians.

Walking up a steep flight of steps behind the stage, one reached a second floor consisting of a long, thin balcony that looked out over the main hall, where people could catch the show from a side angle above the stage. Looking up at the balcony from the ground floor, below the balcony rail one could see a rogue's gallery of posters of the bands that were regulars at D-22, including Joyside, The Scoff, Hedgehog, and P.K.-14. There was also a private room upstairs for bands to hang out and not be bothered by their fans. From there, one could enter onto a small private balcony that looked straight out to the stage ahead and below. Thus, from various vantage points in the club, one could view the bands performing onstage—front, side, and back views, as well as looking down upon them from above. In an interview I had with club founder Michael Pettis, he said this was a club set up mainly to showcase the performing artists, who also made

Michael Pettis during an interview in his office with the author in 2007 (video still from an interview by Andrew Field)

up a sizeable portion of the club's audience on any given night, and to give them a place to hang out, a home away from home.

Michael Pettis and the Formation of D-22

Michael Pettis, a finance expert from Wall Street, came to Beijing in 2002 and decided to stay for a while. By day, he taught finance to graduate students at the Guanghua School of Management in Peking University, and by night he ran D-22. Over the summer and fall of 2007, I spent many nights hanging out there chatting with Michael and his younger partner in this rock club venture, Charles Saliba. Like me, Michael and Charles were both graduates of Columbia University, and Michael once taught in Columbia's School of International and Public Affairs (SIPA). Charles hails from the same hometown as Michael (Malaga, Spain), and was a student of Michael's at Columbia. Not long after settling in China, Michael persuaded Charles to come to Beijing. The two scouted out venues in the area for a rock club. They found one to their liking and opened the club in 2006, with Charles handling most of the day-to-day management tasks. They convinced another young American named Nevin Domer, who had spent a few years in Asia teaching English and playing in a punk rock band, to be the club's booking agent. Charles was tall and thin, with dark hair that had almost disappeared off his balding pate, while Nevin was much shorter, with a boyish face and blond hair.

By the time I arrived in Beijing in the summer of 2007, D-22 had already gained fame in both local and international media as one of the most progressive and nurturing indie rock venues in China. Its location was meant to draw the youthful student population of China's elite universities into that scene, giving them a live taste of indie rock, which theoretically they would then spread to their peers all over China. This was completely intentional on the part of the club's owners. The club was also conveniently within walking distance of Michael Pettis's daytime workplace, Peking University. He also had an office nearby where he, Charles, Nevin and a few other workers did various other things to nurture the nation's indie rock scene to fruition, including setting up a new music label called Maybe Mars.

'I came to China in January 2002, and just found China to be such an exciting place that I decided that I would quit my job and move out here,' said Michael during my interview with him in his office in November 2007. When I asked him how he fell into the music scene, he replied: 'About twenty years ago I used to run a club in New York on the lower East Side on avenue C and 3rd street, and the club specialized in really sort of developing the local music scene, the local East Village music scene. Since then, I've always been involved in the music scene.'

The club that Michael Pettis ran in New York in the early 1980s while earning his MBA from Columbia was called SIN (Safety in Numbers). According to Michael, it was a hole-in-the-wall place with a mic, an amp, and an old bar that probably went back decades. Yet it attracted young progressive rock bands like Sonic Youth, who played in the club along with many other acts from the New York avant-garde rock scene.

Michael Pettis had brown hair that was longer and somewhat tousled on top, and kept much shorter on the sides and back, a habit that probably went back to his days on Wall Street. Under thick eyebrows, his soulful brown eyes had a world-weary sheen to them. When hanging out at the club he often wore simple t-shirts and jeans, like the young rockers in the live music scene, in stark contrast to his formal suit-and-tie appearance on international television when being called upon to speak about China's financial and economic situation. On the day of my interview with him in November 2007, he was wearing a blue

ROCKING THE CHINESE NATION

Champion sweatshirt and faded blue jeans and five-o-clock stubble. He leaned back on a cushy blue sofa in his office, in an office building down the road from the club, gesturing as he talked. Around him the office was stacked with messy piles of posters, boxes, CDs, and other bric-a-brac from the live music scene that he supported.

When I asked Michael what he thought of the music scene in Beijing, he responded: 'From the very beginning I was impressed. It was not a big scene, but it was very sophisticated. There were some really good things happening here, and it was very clear that Beijing had the potential of having a very exciting and important music scene.'

He referenced the large number of artists and bohemian types who congregated in the city. This was a scene that was already quite diverse when Michael Pettis showed up in 2002, with strong grunge, metal, and punk components. There were established indie record labels in Beijing such as Scream and Modern Sky and others such as Bad News Records from Japan, which were already promoting their indie rock bands.

I asked him what else the city's rock scene needed to grow and prosper. He answered: 'There were a couple of things that were lacking. There are a lot of good clubs in Beijing, but for most of the clubs, it's very hard to make money, and they desperately needed to make enough money to stay alive.'

True enough. Just looking at Liu Miao and Gao Feng and their club 2 Kolegas, one could easily see how difficult it was to run an indie rock club that broke even, let alone one that made a sustainable profit. Michael also highlighted another pervasive issue in the Chinese rock scene:

> There's sort of a lack of self-confidence. China's been out of the market for so long, it's been out of the world

for so long, that there's a sense that foreign things are better than local things, that foreign bands get a much bigger draw than good Chinese bands. And so we figured that if we opened a place that had sort of like a New York orientation where the musicians were definitely the stars of the place, had the run of the place and were treated pretty much like the stars, in which we really encouraged musicians to do some of their most radical stuff, stretch, and if there was an audience for it, great. And if there wasn't, it didn't really matter.

D-22 was thus born out of the desire to incubate the scene by creating a welcoming and nurturing environment for China's own budding rock musicians to grow, experiment, and thrive — no matter how big or small the audience might be. In other words, Michael was prepared to take a hit financially on the cost of running the club as long as he succeeded in his ambition of nurturing the rock scene. This way, Michael and Charles and Nevin were able to pick and choose the musicians and bands they liked, whether they drew a crowd or not.

An incubator is a special environment created to provide warmth, nourishment, and safety to bodies that are in the early, tender stages of growth and development. In China's own version of Silicon Valley, all sorts of incubators were nurturing the next generation of gadgets, software, hardware, and app technologies and companies. With its large concentration of universities, research laboratories, and scientific institutions, including the prestigious China Academy of Sciences, the Haidian District was nurturing many of the leading tech companies in China. These included the computer giant Lenovo, as well as Xiaomi, the largest smart phone company to emerge from China, which was conceived in Haidian in 2010. It thus made sense for the district to also be the incubator of other creative scenes such as music. Or at least, it did back in 2007.

'When we first opened up,' recalled Michael, 'we didn't have enough really good bands for all of the weekend and all of the weekday nights that we wanted to book, and we tended to book several bands multiple times a month, but within a year we reached a point where we actually had more than enough bands to keep a really good schedule of shows.'

The long list of bands written on the wall of the D-22 bathroom was a testament to the ability of the club to attract some of Beijing's young up-and-comers in the indie rock scene, as well as veterans of the scene like P.K.-14 and Joyside. How and why were they able to do so? Michael explained:

> Because we've been so supportive of the scene and our club is sort of where all the musicians hang out. They get free drinks, so of course they hang out there, but a lot of them think of the club as sort of like the home base of the Beijing music scene...If we really wanted to develop the Beijing music scene, we knew we had to develop the student audience—that was really key. So by locating ourselves in the university district, it's bad in terms of profits, but it's much easier to get students to come and check out the scene and get their first taste of this music. A lot of them get excited really quickly, they'll come in and say: 'This is weird, what kind of music is this?' And, by the second or third time they're hooked, they're regulars, coming back over and over again...In China, there's a saying that a generation lasts five years—China's been changing so quickly that it seems like every five years is a new generation,

and in the six years I've been in China, I agree. My students six years ago are like fuddy-duddy old men compared to my students today.

Through many site visits in the summer and fall of 2007 and in subsequent years, I did indeed discover that D-22 was a lodestone for musicians and their most loyal fans in the Beijing indie rock scene. Many of the people whom I first met or saw at CH+INDIE Fest in 2 Kolegas were frequenters of D-22 as well. Depending on the time of day or night, it took at least one hour, sometimes a lot longer in heavy traffic, to get from D-22 to 2 Kolegas or vice versa by car. Even getting to the middle of Beijing where the rock club scene was most heavily concentrated was a long haul. If you were a musician, dragging your equipment with you, you were not going to take the subway or bus, which added to the expense, since a taxi ride across town might cost up to 50 yuan (around 8 US dollars at the current exchange rate). For most Chinese musicians and fans, that was a lot of money. Given the distance to Wudaokou from the city center, it took some additional effort and expense to get out there and visit the club,

Flyer for the Punk on Wood concert series at D-22 in July 2007 (courtesy of D-22, property of Andrew Field)
'Punk on Wood' at D22 with Joyside (11 and 18 July 2007)

so those who did tended to be either based here already (i.e., students), or else die-hard fans of the scene, as well as musicians who had been specially invited there by the club managers to be part of that scene.

In July 2007, I paid my first visit to D-22 to catch a series with the intriguing title 'Punk on Wood'. The four-part weekly 'unplugged' series featured local Beijing punk bands Demerit on 4 July, Joyside on 11 July, Casino Demon on 18 July, and The Scoff on 25 July. I had already seen these bands in their full amplified glory at the CH+INDIE Fest, and so I figured it would be an interesting contrast to see them stripped down to their acoustic undergarments. Well, not completely — as it turned out, some of their instruments were electric and were hooked up to amps, but the spirit of the concert was 'unplugged'.

I first checked out the Joyside show on 11 July. Lead singer 'Billy' Bian Yuan (also known as Shang Huanhuan and probably a few other names as well), sporting bright pink pantaloons with

Joyside lead singer Billy Bian (Bian Yuan) performing solo at D-22 during the Punk on Wood 'unplugged' concert series in July 2007 (photo by Andrew Field)

black guitar pick designs on them, and his usual funky pimp hat, performed a solo set featuring songs by David Bowie ('Five Years'), the Kinks ('Sunny Afternoon'), the Rolling Stones ('As Tears Go By'), and other classics. The following Wednesday, 18 July, I was back at D-22 to watch Casino Demon, but they ended up not showing up at the last minute, and instead Bian Yuan was called upon to entertain the crowd.

It was a revelation to see Joyside's lead singer with his long hair hanging over his eyes strumming on a red electric guitar and playing from memory a series of old rock tunes from the '60s, '70s, '80s, and '90s, some of which were unfamiliar to me. This time he was joined by another Chinese guitarist wearing camouflage shorts and a Beavis and Butthead t-shirt, who came on stage with an acoustic guitar, a pack of smokes, and a beer. They played a particularly soulful rendition of the Guns N' Roses song 'You Can't Put Your Arms Around a Memory' and followed that with 'Lonely Planet Boy' by the New York Dolls. They also performed an anti-Vietnam protest anthem, P.F. Sloan's 1965 hit 'Eve of Destruction', which gave the concert and the club a folksy Greenwich Village feel.

While their songs elicited a mixed response from the crowd — at one point, somebody, perhaps a rival band member, yelled out 'Boring!' — the event brought out a tender and even vulnerable side to the otherwise wild punk rock singer, whose drunken, raging, devil-may-care on-stage persona was well-known in the scene. Few were there to witness this intimate performance — perhaps only a dozen or so guests. According to Michael Pettis, Joyside was one of the key bands that he and his club were nurturing. Indeed, it was hard to imagine Bian Yuan pulling off this soft acoustic set at 2 Kolegas or anywhere else in town.

Through the 'Punk on Wood' concerts, I discovered that there was more depth to the musical knowledge of Joyside's lead singer than I imagined the first time I saw them at the CH+INDIE Fest at 2 Kolegas. Indeed, it turned out that they were in the middle of recording an album called *Booze at Neptune's Dawn*, which was somewhat more contemplative, melodic, and lyrical than their previous piss-and-beer-and-smokes punk anthems. Not surprisingly, Michael Pettis was nurturing this new album as well, and later that year it came out as one of the debut albums on his new label Maybe Mars.

According to Michael Pettis, the rock scene he was nurturing at D-22 was indicative of broader social and political forces that were mounting in China. 'A lot of people compare our club to CBGB's,' Michael told me. 'They say it really feels like New York or London in the mid to late '70s, and in some ways it does but I really think it more like San Francisco maybe in the mid '60s, in that there was a real social change going on.'

Sure enough, in both the local and international media, comparisons of D-22 to CBGBs were rife. CBGBs was the club in New York City where punk and new wave bands like the Ramones, Blondie, the B-52s, and Talking Heads and others first made a name for themselvesin the late 1970s and early 1980s. Still, it was hard to imagine that these Beijing bands would ever reach the same level of popularity as their CBGB counterparts in the foreseeable future. Instead, they would have to remain content with being the heroes of the local Chinese rock scene. For a city of well over 10 million, and a district featuring some of China's top universities, that was a huge accomplishment in and of itself.

'A lot of real creative stuff is happening here [in Beijing],' Michael continued. '[We see] musicians that are going to have a big impact, not just on the development of the Chinese scene, but also have an impact abroad, and new stuff coming out of here. In certain areas in think Beijing is already about as good as almost any city in the world.' I asked him how the scene compared to New York. His reply:

> This [scene] reminds me of New York in the early '80s. There's just so much stuff happening, all these people trying new things. And, maybe most importantly, [we wanted] to bring the support of foreign critics and foreign institutions to sort of help pull that self-confidence, and we thought that we might see something really interesting develop here. So we were really happy to see that the scene was just so ready, that once we opened up it exploded, and since then a number of other clubs have opened up and a couple of different scenes have developed.

The Metal Scene at 13 Club in Wudaokou
Located amidst a cluster of Chinese restaurants half a kilometer west of Wudaokou towards the campus of Peking University was 13 Club, the next-door neighbor of the club D-22. The founder and manager was Liu Lixin, a former PLA soldier who formed a metal band in 1999 called Ordnance (军械所). While not overtly anti-government, the band's albums and lyrics were full of social critiques — one song is called 'Fuck You (Police)!'. In an online interview Liu Lixin said that his band's albums were banned from sales in record shops and airplay on the radio, but that they circulated widely through the 'underground grassroots and grapevine' metal scene. Opening in 2004, 13 Club became a favored venue for metal rockers and their fans, attracting a fair number of prominent metal bands in the scene. The club was small and stuffy, decorated with a mishmash of typical pub designs and graffiti, and it featured an elevated stage.

Closeup shot of two members of the band Evil Thorn performing in 13 Club on 4 Aug 2007 (photo by Andrew Field)

Evil Thorn at 13 Club (4 August 2007)

On the night of Tuesday, 4 August, while visiting neighboring club D-22 to catch the Carsick Cars and other bands (see Chapter 2) I also went to the 13 Club to see a metal concert featuring seven different bands. Because I spent most of the night at D-22, I was only able to catch the final act, a Chinese band called Evil Thorn. The band members of this all-male band were decked out with white makeup on their faces and black around the eyes. They all had long, straight hair, and they wore black leather outfits with plenty of metal spikes and other accoutrements. The lead singer sported an impressive pair of spikey armbands on his arms. As expected, the music was loud and heavy, with the band members strumming power chords on their amped-up guitars.

What captured my attention was not so much their music but rather the on-stage theatrics of the band, who took up positions at the front of the stage. As they strummed their power chords, resting one foot atop the amps at the front of the stage, they rolled their heads, made faces, and stuck out their tongues at the audience. Near the front of the stage, a whole cadre of youthful Chinese metal fans were shaking their heads up and down in classic 'headbanger' fashion to the music. They raised their hands in a 'devil horns' salute to the music. One lone foreigner tried to mosh — an act more typical of punk and indie concerts than metal ones — and he was soon told by another audience member to stop. The scene on stage that night reminded me of Peking Opera with its flashy acrobatics and actors heavily made up and in colorful costumes. Or perhaps it was a sort of exorcism ritual, which one might liken to men painted up as demons in ancient village rites.

After the concert ended, the band members all headed backstage to change their outfits and remove their makeup. We then joined them at a nearby restaurant that served *shaokao* barbequed veggies and skewered meats, known in the Beijing dialect as *chuanr* 串. It turned out that two of the band members were working by day in the office of a music company that an American friend of mine ran in Beijing. It was he who invited me to join the concert that evening, hence our invitation to the after-party.

Over a late-night meal, I spent some time talking to the guitarist 南山 'South Mountain,' a large and solid fellow who fit the moniker he was given. While we chatted about the Chinese music scene, his girlfriend combed his raven locks with great care, and then she moved on to do the same for his bandmates. While the band put on a great demonic act on stage, offstage they were courteous and chatty, steadily working their way through piles of *chuanr* washed down with copious bottles of local beer as they were groomed by Nanshan's attentive girlfriend. This all left me with a lasting impression of the staginess and the camaraderie and cultivated masculinity of men who were part of the metal rock scene.

As to be expected, the metal scenes nurtured in clubs like Yugong Yishan and 13 Club displayed an adherence to the global norms of metal culture, while also taking on certain 'Chinese characteristics' in terms of the sounds, lyrics, styles, and tastes of the musicians and their fans. These bands were tightly networked together through the friendships of the musicians, through bonding over food and drink at local eateries, and through concerts that brought them onto the stage with other metal bands in China.

The Punk Scene at MAO Livehouse
Another Beijing indie rock scene could be found in a midtown venue called MAO Live House. Located a few hundred meters east of the old Drum Tower, *gulou*, one of the icons of Imperial Beijing, MAO Live House occupied a former cinema. When I arrived in the city in summer 2007, it had not been there very long. It opened earlier that February, making it a recent and welcome addition to the city's live music scene. The founder was a Beijinger named Li Chi, a rock music buff and former record shop owner. Backing the club was Bad News Records, an indie/punk record label from Japan, and the club was built on a Japanese live house model. With its more advanced sound system and cavernous club space fitting in as many as 800 people, MAO quickly built up a reputation in town as one of the leading clubs for both up-and-coming and veteran indie rock musicians, especially those who dominated the punk scene such as the notorious band Brain Failure (脑浊). While it did not have the experimental cachet as D-22, nor the grungy DIY feel of 2 Kolegas, there was still significant overlap among the bands that played at those two clubs and those that played at MAO Live House. Over the summer and fall of 2007, I spent more time

and saw more bands at MAO Live House than at any other rock music club in town. I came to think of MAO Live House as the 'beating heart' of the Beijing punk and indie scenes.

The club was located on 111 Gulou East Street, right across from the northern entrance to the heavily commercialized north-south running alleyway known as Nanluoguxiang 南锣鼓巷. This was a busy, noisy nightlife neighborhood full of shops, including music shops selling guitars and other instruments, as well as countless small restaurants, eateries, and bars that were open until late night. It was just west of the famous restaurant road known as 'Ghost Street' (鬼街), lined with gaudy neon-and-fluorescent-lit hotpot and seafood restaurants that truly were open all night.

A few hundred meters west of the club, the street opened into the intersection with Di'anmen Outer Street, a broad avenue that runs on the north-south meridian from the Forbidden City to the Drum Tower, making it one of the most sacred pathways in all of China during Beijing's long and glorious epoch as the imperial capital of the realm. The magnificent red building of the Drum Tower stands tall and proud on the northern part of this intersection, with its multiple eaves painted and decorated with imperial green, blue and yellow designs. Many of the most famous hutong neighborhoods in Beijing, some dating back to the Mongol Yuan dynasty, are encompassed in the view from atop the Drum Tower or the neighboring Bell Tower. The hutong aesthetic with its narrow alleys filled with small, single-story courtyard homes made of brick pervaded this area and set the tone for the neighborhood.

MAO Live House was composed of two parts. A more colorful outer area containing a bricked-up bar, an old foosball table, some beat-up sofas, and a hallway with more seating wrapped around the inner core of the club. Inside that core was a walled-in performance space, painted all in black, with a stage that prominently displayed the logo of the club, a slightly abstract yet obvious rendition of the outline of Chairman Mao's famous head, with sun rays radiating from it. The two layers of the club walls kept the music inside from bothering neighborhood residents and businesses outside the club. You could barely hear the music from the street. The effect of the two layers of the club also seemed to resonate with the multi-layered, labyrinthine quality of the centuries-old neighborhood that surrounded and enveloped the club. This gave it an aura of secrecy, which might be likened to an ancient cave temple, in which sacred rites were being performed behind closed and closely guarded doors.

While the dark and womblike interior of the club at times felt claustrophobic and even dangerous when it held a large crowd, there was also a feeling of security inside the black walls of the club. MAO Live House really felt like a 'scene,' in the true sense of the word: a large and bubbling congregation of people from diverse backgrounds and areas, who came together to celebrate their common love for music. While punk rock seemed to be the dominant music of the scene, the club served as a hangout for a wide range of musicians, and its programming was even more eclectic than either D-22 or 2 Kolegas. It also regularly featured foreign acts coming to Beijing to perform.

The central location of the club in the city helped attract a diverse crowd from both eastern and western districts. Other distinctions include the acoustics, the sound system, and the size of the venue. It still had an intimate feel to it, unlike some of the larger music clubs such as Starlive, a live music hall just north of the Lama Temple, which could easily fit 1,000 or more people. The only club that felt and looked somewhat comparable size-wise was the new Yugong Yishan club, which also opened in 2007 in a central location just a few blocks south from this neighborhood.

MAO Live House was also a club where audience members displayed the signature dances of punk and hardcore music. With its relatively large yet still intimate stage-audience nexus, the club offered plenty of room for a mosh pit to grow in the center of the floor near the stage. The size of the mosh pit and the number of moshers—young people, men for the most part, throwing their bodies around and bumping joyously, aggressively, and playfully into each other—varied with the band and the performance. Sometimes there was only a small handful of youths—usually males—dancing around near the stage, and at other times it felt like half the audience had entered the swirling, whirling vortex of the mosh pit.

Ramones Tribute Concert at MAO (3 August 2007)
My first visit to MAO Live House was on the night of Friday, 3 August, 2007. I headed there to join in a celebration of the American godfathers of punk rock: The Ramones. The concert was a warm-up and a promotional event for the upcoming Beijing Pop Festival in September, which would feature drummer Marky Ramone along with the New York Dolls and many other legendary rock bands. The Ramones tribute concert at MAO Live House featured Beijing punk indie rock bands including Joyside, Demerit, SKO, Guai Li, and the New Pants.

On this night, Brain Failure's lead singer Xiao Rong made a surprise appearance during the New Pants concert. With his signature leopard-print hair and a black leather jacket to go with the punk theme of the night, he sang as the rate of moshing grew exponentially. The song that they played was the Ramones' 'The KKK Took my Baby Away'. The audience had already been revved up by the band known as the New Pants (新裤子), whose songs, usually sung in Mandarin Chinese, were so well known by the crowd that most of the audience was singing along to them. Suddenly, Xiao Rong burst out on stage waving his arms up and down as the crowd broke into joyful cheers and chanted out his name. He took up his guitar and joined the members of the New Pants in performing the song, starting out with a collective drumbeat-fueled chant of dadadadada...'Hey!' dadadadada... 'Hey!', hundreds of arms and fists raised together in punk style, and going ahead with the song as the entire crowd erupted into the most energetic moshing and pogoing frenzy that I had yet seen in Beijing. The moshing also seemed to be a way for Chinese and foreign rock fans to come together in a playful bout of camaraderie and temporary social bonding, much as they did in an earlier age on the cavernous disco dance floors of Beijing and Shanghai.

Guns N' Roses Tribute Concert at MAO (10 August 2007)
I returned to MAO Live House the following Friday, August 10, this time to witness a Guns N' Roses tribute concert. The night's headliners were Ziyo, the band fronted by Chinese American singer Helen Feng, and Brain Failure. The club took on a friendly and convivial community feeling as I hung out with Dirty Deeds front man Jaime Welton and a few other Americans at the bar, including Jaime's bandmate Dez, the singer in another blues-based Beijing band Jaime played in called Black Cat Bone. We were downing shots of whiskey, surrounded by a sizeable crowd of people of all sorts milling in and out of the concert hall itself, either to refuel with drinks or to take a break from the bands.

After a few shots, the outer part of the club took on a cave-like feel with its red walls and bathroom stalls festooned with colorful calligraphy, primitive drawings, and carved messages. It reminded me of the cave paintings of Lascaux and made one think of all the rituals that must have gone on in those ancient

European caves thirty thousand years ago, rituals that no doubt involved plenty of drums, flutes, and other musical instruments, and perhaps even magic mushrooms or other psychedelic herbs, bringing together the various clans in the region along with their shamans for a mind-bending night of song, dance, pleasure, magic, and ecstasy.

While Helen Feng and her band Ziyo put on a great show that night, choosing 'Sweet Child 'o Mine' as their tribute to GnR, the highlight of the evening was Brain Failure, the final band on the roster. That band seemed to own this club, figuratively if not literally. It is no coincidence that their Japanese label, Bad News Records, was also heavily invested in the club. The band consisted of lead singer and guitarist Xiao Rong with his trademark leopard skin hair, along with guitarist Wang Jian who was sporting a tall and spikey Mohawk and a long pointy goatee, bassist Ma Jiliang who had short hair and a red t-shirt, and drummer Xu Lin.

Brain Failure's lead singer Xiao Rong with his trademark leopard-print hairdo performing at MAO Live House on Aug 10, 2007 (photo by Andrew Field)

ROCKING THE CHINESE NATION

Brain Failure began their act with a repetitive droning loop of guitar and bass as Ma Jiliang and Wang Jian took the stage, lit by an eerie blue light. Eventually Xiao Rong came out of the backstage to join them, and on cue the lights came on full blast and they burst out into their opening song, 'Coming Down to Beijing.' This was Brain Failure's anthem to the city and I would hear it again many times, including at the Beijing Pop Festival in September. The song had a manic energy as expected from a punk band that took its cues from The Clash and The Ramones. The frenetic, kinetic energy of the band as they strummed their guitars rapidly and leapt about on stage was immediately transferred to the audience, with dozens of youths of many nationalities dancing close to the stage, separated from the musicians by a squad of photographers and videographers trying to get close-ups of the band members.

As Xiao Rong broke into the opening verse of the song, Chinese and western youths crowded up to the front of the stage, faces lit up in huge grins, and with their arms up and hands pointing in time to his verse. As he hit the chorus, everyone in the house chanted 'B-E-I-J-I-N-G.' The song was a paean to the city in all its glory, reminding us of the grand history, the immortal palaces, lakes, and parks, but also of the rapid development, the destruction of the ancient *hutong* neighborhoods, the dirt, the grime, the smog, the noise, the dust, and the tall new buildings rising out of the mud and death of the old. It was the soundtrack to the city's fast-paced rebuilding phase as it made itself up for the upcoming Olympics, and at the same time it was a harbinger for the 'red alert' smog days and sandstorms coming down the pipeline in the years ahead, as China wrestled with its environmental crises. But on this night, everyone was just rocking out and having fun, moving their bodies to the rhythms of Brain Failure as they chanted out one song after another, until the whole scene was just one sweaty, whirling mass of bodies and voices chanting in unison. Afterwards, many people including myself and the band members of Black Cat Bone spilled out of the club for a breath of 'fresh air' and made our way across the street to Nanluoguxiang for a late-night snack of *chuanr*.

Beijing's Rock Club Scenes: A Reprisal

In 2007 and the years to follow, the scenes at Yugong Yishan, 13 Club, 2 Kolegas, D-22, and MAO Live House collectively defined the indie rock music culture of the city more than any other venues. While larger stages such as the club Starlive or the big music festivals (which I describe later in this book) featured more prominent acts, they lacked the tight, tribal, intimate focus and experimental nature of these clubs with their dedicated musicians and fan bases. These clubs each nurtured distinctive music scenes, though admittedly there was significant overlap, since many of the bands that were more active in Beijing played in all the clubs at some point or other. Nevertheless, the bands, gigs, and concert festivals these clubs supported were largely driven by the interests and tastes of the club owners and promoters as well as their personal connections with different bands. They brought the bands and their fans together in a common milieu through the primitive rituals of drinking, smoking, singing, and dancing on the floor of the club in unison. Bands congregated in these clubs to meet, compete, share musical ideas, and learn from each other. Fans, whether Chinese or foreign, were there to experience the highs of discovering, witnessing, and nurturing creative, noisy, and experimental musical scenes in China.

2

LEADING VOICES: CONCERTS AND CONVERSATIONS WITH CHINESE INDIE ROCKERS

IN 2007, several bands from the Beijing indie rock scene were emerging into the limelight and sharing that light with veteran bands of the scene. This chapter aims to represent the voices, sounds, and styles of some of Beijing's leading and aspiring indie rock bands during that vital period in the development of indie rock in China. Topics discussed in my interviews with these musicians included their personal backgrounds and their journeys into the Beijing rock scenes, the development of their styles, their songwriting techniques, processes, and methods, as well as their philosophies and attitudes towards music and towards society. Overall, I conclude that, not surprisingly, their voices represented a rebellious attitude of leading indie rock musicians in China towards sources of conformity, authority, and power. These sources range from their own parents to schools, government, media, and the recording industry itself. Their music, which was noisy and unusual, even for the indie rock scene, and certainly far from what people would consider 'mainstream' in any definable genre, reflected their anti-establishment philosophies. In other words, these bands were rebelling against the more conventional sounds and styles either of pop music in general or of more established rock bands in

Beijing—even the punk bands that had paved the way for their own rise in the Beijing scenes.

Rising Stars: Guai Li, Hedgehog, and Carsick Cars at D-22 (4 August 2007)

One of the bands that was prominent in Beijing's indie rock scene in 2007 was Carsick Cars. When I arrived on the scene that summer, the band was already being touted in the local media and in some international media outlets as one of the top indie rock acts in China. At the time, many people were comparing Carsick Cars' distinctive sound with the US indie/experimental band Sonic Youth, and it turned out they had an ongoing relationship. Michael Pettis knew the New York-based band Sonic Youth from his days running the SIN club in the East Village, where they performed in the early 1980s. Carsick Cars were supposed to open for Sonic Youth at a concert in Beijing in April 2007, but the government mysteriously decided to cancel that concert at the last minute. Later that year, in August, they opened for Sonic Youth in August in Prague and Vienna. This was the start of a promising journey of this young Chinese rock band onto the international rock concert circuit.

Many at the time were talking about the lead singer and songwriter of the band, Zhang Shouwang.

'Carsick Cars is driven pretty much completely by the interests of Shouwang,' said Michael to me 2007. '[He is] maybe one of the most important young musicians in the world. He's already been called, much to his dismay—he hates this—by a number of musicians as maybe the first genius of Chinese music, or of modern Chinese music.'

To be sure, this was a grandiose claim, and perhaps there was a fair bit of self-promotion behind it. After all, Carsick Cars was to Michael Pettis what Lonely China Day was to Matt Kagler:

ROCKING THE CHINESE NATION

It was the marquee band both of his club D-22 and of his new record label Maybe Mars.

Even so, not too long after I showed up at D-22 to see my first Carsick Cars show, music critic Alex Ross visited the club on a tour of China, and later added Shouwang's solo performance at D-22 to a top-ten list of musical performances for the year 2008 in his *New Yorker* magazine column on December 5, describing him as 'the brilliant young guitarist-composer Zhang Shouwang casting a minimalist spell in a Beijing rock club.'

'The first night I went to D-22 [to see Carsick Cars], Zhang [Shouwang] performed a solo piece that featured beguiling minimalist patterns over steady drones, moving purposefully from clean, simple harmonies into duskier, more chromatic regions. In time-honored Led Zeppelin fashion, Zhang played the guitar strings with a violin bow, to which he meticulously applied rosin beforehand,' writes Ross in another *New Yorker* article published on 7 July 2008 on classical music in China. Michael Pettis was very proud of these references in one of America's most prestigious magazines, rightly so, and later he mentioned it to me more than once.

'And, in that area,' Michael continued, '[Shouwang is] really experimenting a lot with noise, he's really one of the most exciting guitar players I've ever seen, and in that sense, there's sort of no clear line between rock and what you may want to call avant-garde, experimental, whatever that stuff is called.'

My first opportunity to see Carsick Cars perform was in August, 2007. Held on a sweltering Saturday night, the triple lineup of 'hot bands' Carsick Cars, Hedgehog, and Guai Li attracted people from all over the city to witness D-22 at the height of its powers as the city's leading incubator of Chinese indie rock. I had already seen Hedgehog perform at CH+INDIE Fest at 2 Kolegas, and I was looking forward to seeing them again. I had also been waiting to see the much-touted band Carsick Cars perform for a while now. They were getting plenty of coverage in the local expat magazines in Beijing.

'Carsick Cars is in many ways the most talked about and respected band in China right now,' Michael Pettis told me later. Judging from the talk of the town and the local news media, these two bands were on everyone's radar screen as *the* bands to see. Guai Li was also a new band that people in the scene were raving about. Like SUBS, the band was given a vague 'post-punk' label and it also featured a female lead singer named Wen Jun.

I arrived at D-22 around 9:30 pm to find a sizeable crowd gathering outside the club entrance. This was a much bigger crowd than I had seen at the club to date. I recognized some musicians, including the three members of Hedgehog: Atom, Z.O., and BoX. They were just hanging around, smoking, and chatting with other musicians and with their fans. I also recognized a lot of other folks, Chinese and foreigners, whom I identified as habitues of the indie rock scene. With Mohawks and other punkish hairstyles, and with ear, nose, and face piercings, funky hats, and other identification markers, they stood out from the other members of the crowd who were less committed to the indie music scene.

Among the people outside the club entrance was a tall, rail-thin Chinese woman with long hair colored bright orange. Her hair partially covered her eyes, giving her that mysterious look typical to some punk rockers. She was wearing a pair of faded black jeans and a long-sleeve silken collared shirt covered with squares of small purple crosses surrounded by blue-and-white tiles. Upon closer inspection it looked like alternations of blue-and-white square tubes chained together on a purple background. She was standing alone against the backdrop of the crowd, smoking a cigarette and brooding. Somebody identified her as Wen Jun, the lead singer of the band Guai Li. After finishing her cigarette, she went into the club and got busy preparing with her band to perform. After the usual long tune-up and sound check, they begin their performance at around 10:30 pm. This was going to be a long night.

At this point in the evening, the crowd appeared to be largely Chinese, with a smattering of foreigners. The ratio would change over the long night, as always seemed to happen with the rock club scene, and foreigners would come to predominate. While most of these youths were not 'punked up', they wore fun t-shirts with random messages in English, including some Ramones t-shirts, which seemed to represent an initial and tentative foray into the Bohemian world of the indie rock club scene. Many of them were students from the nearby universities, including Peking and Tsinghua University as well as many others. In this respect, Michael Pettis's aim to attract Chinese university students into the scene was apparently meeting with some success.

Guai Li

Later, when I asked Michael Pettis about the band Guai Li, he told me: 'They put this band together, and from the very beginning we thought this is a band we're going to get behind, because they're a band we think are going to make an awful lot of noise on the scene in the next few years.' Guai Li was one of the newer bands on the scene that Michael Pettis and club D-22 were incubating, and that night Michael and Charles were there to witness this special performance. In addition to the tall, willowy lead singer Wen Jun, the band featured two guitarists, a bassist, and a drummer. The guitarists were Xu Sheng and Liu Yue. He Yifan was the bassist and the drummer Shi Xudong. He was new to the band, since their previous drummer left in 2006. Nevertheless, he was the most experienced member of the

Guai Li and their lead singer Wen Jun performing at D-22 on 4 Aug 2007 (photo by Andrew Field)

band, having played in many other indie punk bands in Beijing over the years, including SUBS (Shi Xudong was one of SUBS' founding members, and he drummed for the band from their origins in 2002 until 2006). Tall and thin, with short-cropped hair, and tautly muscular, he was an awesome presence on the drums, and not only that—he was also the bassist for the band P.K. 14.

The band Guai Li, who associated their name with witchcraft and dark magic, launched into their first song. From the start, the music was harsh, dissonant, strident, bizarre, and haunting, but also structured and methodical. Xu Shidong provided a powerful beat that anchored the rest of the band. The guitarists were accomplished with their instruments, and they provided some good licks, with a hard-rock feel to them but also some strange echoing riffs kind of like a surfer band hired for a Halloween party. Wen Jun was singing her songs with a lilting, chanting voice that moved up and down the register from a growl to a squeal, reminding me of some of the punk goddesses from the late 1970s and early 1980s. Her thick lips caressed the microphone as she sang, threatening to swallow it whole every now and then.

Unlike Kang Mao of SUBS, Wen Jun did not indulge her crowd in a highly theatrical performance. Her bodily performance on stage was tight and conservative, but her singing was punctuated now and then with a high-pitched scream as the band erupted into a noisy crescendo. As she sang into the mic, she stood tall and held herself close to the microphone, her eyes almost totally covered by her bangs. She often closed her eyes as if she was deep in concentration. She seemed to be singing in English, although the lyrics were very hard to identify. The guitarists echoed her voice with some cool riffs that sounded ghostly and strange, like the band's name. At times, her voice sounded hurt and angry, like a spurned lover. But in one more upbeat and 'fun' piece, she picked up a green melodica — a small, handheld keyboard with an air tube — and played it by blowing into the tube, adding to the funky cacophony that the band was making. Gathered as close as possible to the stage, the largely Chinese student audience watched this performance of musical noise with great intensity, and there was little if any dancing.

One question that people often ask is why so many Chinese indie rock bands choose the English language as their medium of expression. After Guai Li's set ended, another American and I were chatting outside the club about the bands in Beijing and he brought up this question. I figured it this was one we should ask the bands directly, so we walked over to Wen Jun and the band's guitarists and shot them the question. They explained that the music goes much better with English lyrics than with Chinese. I asked them if the tonal system of Chinese makes it difficult to pair the language with the music they play, and they agreed that this was indeed the case. Kang Mao, the lead singer of SUBS, said something similar when I asked her the same question while interviewing her. Yet there are many other reasons as well for choosing the English language for their songs. In addition to the tonality of the language, the bands were more accustomed to hearing rock music in English, so it made sense for them to draw from an English vocabulary when creating their own songs, especially if that process is partly a subconscious one. Another motivating factor was their desire to reach an international audience both inside and outside of China. Wen Jun agreed to do a more extensive interview with me, though it was not until later that fall that I was able to catch up with her again. Meanwhile, there were two more hot bands to round off the night at D-22.

Hedgehog

After talking with Wen Jun and her fellow band members, we headed back into the club to catch the next act, Hedgehog (刺猬). Later, when I asked Michael Pettis why this band was on his A-list, he replied: 'Hedgehog is a band that started roughly around the same time as those other bands did, and the drummer [Atom] is a little girl who is just one of the most powerful drummers

Bo Xuan (l) and Zi Jian (r) of the band Hedgehog performing at D-22 on 4 Aug 2007 while drummer Atom is in the background (photo by Andrew Field)

in China. Everyone was blown away by her, and suddenly they became the hottest band in Beijing.' Tag Team Records owner Matt Kagler agreed with Michael: 'Yeah, Hedgehog are great. The cutest band in China, hands down.'

Hedgehog began the set with their song 'Toy & 61 Festival.' The songs from their first album have a childish feel to them. Accompanied by a jolly, sweet tune that sounds like it could be an American children's breakfast cereal jingle from the 1970s, and with vocal backing and harmonization from drummer Atom, lead singer Z.O. sang about running and jumping in the blue sky and about wanting to be a 'bad boy'. It is a naïve and fun song with a touch of naughtiness to it. The song seems to be about a loss of childish innocence and the wish to regain it, tensioned with the desire to move on to the next stage of life. For a group of young twenty-somethings beginning the long trek into full adulthood, it was a fitting sentiment. With the drummer Atom singing with him both on the album and in their live performances, Z.O. sang the song in recognizable English, so that a person with the lyric sheet could easily follow along.

That night, on the small intimate stage of D-22, the band was giving the audience a huge dose of rock energy. As they played their instruments, the two young men in the band jumped around the stage with great zest. Z.O. was wearing the typical outfit of a white t-shirt and black jeans, while BoX had on a white tank top, showing off his thin yet muscular shoulders as he handled his instrument. Atom had on a lacey black dress with an open v-neck as she played the drums at the back of the stage. Z.O. went into a long solo that kept the main hook going with some extra *umph* added. He was playing a yellow electric guitar. BoX's bass guitar was a shiny turquoise color. 'I love play my toy,' sang Z.O. as he slashed into his yellow guitar, taking an occasional frenzied solo that departed from the main melody into the realm of dissonant noise.

The band labelled its own sound 'noisepop.' This was indeed a fitting term for its sound. During their song 'Noise Hit World', Atom started screaming into the mic at one point in the song, after the chorus. At one point during another song, Z.O.'s solo morphed into an industrial rage, totally removed from the pop tune that they were playing—more Nine Inch Nails than The Cure. His hair covered his eyes and sweaty face as he chanted or yelled the lyrics, ending the song with a Robert Smith-like 'yeow' as the crowd erupted into applause and cheers.

Carsick Cars

By midnight, the crowd at D-22 was much larger. Well over 200 people had poured into the club to see the band Carsick Cars. Many more were hanging out just outside the club. Many audience members were foreigners, and while some appeared to be students from the nearby universities, others looked somewhat older and more conventional in their appearance

A young crowd of Chinese and foreign fans, including the band members of Hedgehog (right near stage) watch intensely as Zhang Shouwang (l) and his band Carsick Cars perform at D-22 on 4 Aug 2007 (video still by Andrew Field)

than the youthful Bohemian types who normally frequented the scene. Apparently, these were people who had made the journey over to Wudaokou from the eastern district of Chaoyang where they worked in embassies, schools, or corporate offices. The area in front of the stage was absolutely jam-packed with people, and many others looked down on the stage from the upstairs balcony as the trio began their performance.

Fronting the band was the young guitarist and singer Zhang Shouwang, who also went by the English name of Jeffray. He was slightly built, with a large, squarish face and furry brows, framed by tousled hair that, like Michael Pettis, was longer on top and shorter around the ears (except that his hair was also neck-length at the back). On his lip was a feathery thin mustache that made him look like an adolescent. He wore a black t-shirt that looked to be two sizes too large for him, with a red-and-white cartoon-like design on the chest that read 'welcome to your dream'. He strummed an old Gibson SG cherry wood electric guitar, with a capo placed at the sixth fret. His chords were simple, but the strumming was lightning fast, rhythmic, and hypnotic.

Beside him was bassist Li Weisi, who wore his hair in a Beatlesque mop and sported the Rolling Stones red-lips-and-tongue icon on his white t-shirt. Behind them was female drummer Li Qing. She was wearing a white-black-red striped button-down collared short-sleeved shirt, had similar hair to the bassist. They opened with a song that I would later recognize as 'Volunteer' (志愿的人) from their first album released in 2007 on the Maybe Mars label. Shouwang started out the song with a folksy guitar hook that reminded me of the American rock band R.E.M. from their early days, but it quickly became more frantic. There was no fancy guitar work here, no masterful solos to delight the crowd. Rather, the guitar work of Zhang Shouwang consisted of lightning-fast yet simple bar-chord strumming up and down the fret board, along with some distortion added to give the guitar a harsh, grating, crying, metallic, industrial sound. This was not the studied musicianship of a conservatory graduate, nor the showmanship of a rock guitar hero. Still, there was a method behind the madness of Shouwang's guitar playing. Several different guitar effects pedals colored in green, red, white, and black were lined up in front of his feet, and he used them all in turn.

As Zhang Shouwang played his Gibson, he sang—chanted is more like it—the song 'Volunteer' in Mandarin. The lyrics are deceivingly simple, but like the music behind them, they are seething with dissonant and perhaps even dissident meanings. The term 'volunteer' (志愿) is laden with political meaning in China. Shouwang sang about an anonymous 'volunteer' who donates his wife, child, property, arms, and brain. To whom exactly he is giving these things, the song does not specify. Perhaps the yellow hat worn by the 'volunteer' in the song suggested the helmets worn by teams of construction workers, who flocked from the provinces to build China's big cities. If you headed over to the eastern Chaoyang district of the city during this period in the leadup to the 2008 Beijing Olympics, you would see thousands of these construction workers working, living, and even sleeping on site to build the high new towers that were going up in the city's financial district. These towers included the oddly designed CCTV Building nicknamed 'the Pants,' which was halfway towards completion, although yet to be joined by the bridge at the top, so it looks like two towers sticking out in odd directions. They were also building the tallest building in Beijing, dubbed the new Financial Tower.

One could easily read a critique or even a parody of socialism into Shouwang's lyrics. Back in the Mao years, Lei Feng, a young soldier in the People's Liberation Army, was the poster boy for selfless sacrifice to the Party and the People. Where were the Lei Fengs of this new age, the selfless heroes willing to sacrifice their personal comforts and possessions and volunteer for the common good? Perhaps they were the nameless millions of common laborers, who quietly 'volunteered' their bodies to build the edifices in which China's rich disported themselves, sacrificing years of time with their families though supporting them in the provincial heartlands to do so. Since they did not have proper *hukou* or residence permits allowing them to live and work in the city, these migrant laborers couldn't reap the benefits of urban life such as housing, education, and social services, and so they left their families behind and donated their brawn and their brains to the building of the new China. Other than on the noisy, dusty construction sites, there was no life and no future for these men in the big city. If they were lucky, they slept in crudely built bunkhouses; or they slept outside on site in their underwear on the hard, dusty, ground.

Whether or not this was indeed the inspiration to the lyrics of the song, the meaning and import of the lyrics of 'Volunteers' were mostly lost on this largely foreign crowd of people, who were at D-22 to witness something unusual in the performance itself. And they got what they came for with the next song. Zhang Shouwang grabbed a drumstick and applied it to his guitar strings, drawing it back and forth across the strings like a violin bow in a tremolo action near the sound hole, and thereby creating a demonic, high-pitched, rising, grating, shrieking sound that sounded like a noisy construction site. Li Weisi accompanied him with a low, ominous lick on the bass, while Li Qing continued to keep time on the drums from the back of the stage. The sound was deafening and many of the people in the audience were cupping their ears. Others were watching closely, mesmerized with the work of this young Chinese artist, a rising star in the global firmament of indie music. The performance ended in a frenetic crescendo, and with a flick of his arm and wrist, Shouwang sent the drumstick scuttling across the fret board to end the song amidst cheers and loud applause. A bravura performance. This was truly avant-garde work in China's indie rock scene. Whereas Kang Mao, the lead singer of SUBS, gave her primal scream with her own voice, Shouwang did it with his instrument. Later, I would identify this song as 'Gum', the second song to appear on their first album, produced by Michael Pettis's record label, Maybe Mars.

Veterans of the Indie Rock Scene: P.K. 14 at MAO Live House (9 November 2007)

Over the summer and fall of 2007, I had been hearing a great deal about a band called P.K. 14, one of the legends of China's indie rock scene. I finally had the chance to see them perform in November of that year. On this night, P.K. 14 was the only act

Lead singer Yang Haisong performs at MAO Live House with his band P.K. 14 on 9 Nov 2007. Behind him is guitarist Xu Bo (photo by Andrew Field)

performing in the club. This was unusual, since normally there were several bands booked on any given night. Perhaps it was a testament to the popularity of the band that they were able to fill the MAO Live House entirely on their own.

In addition to lead singer Yang Haisong, P.K. 14 had three other members. Xu Bo, the guitarist, was a thickset man with a schoolboy's bowl cut and a chubby face. That night he was wearing a white collared long-sleeve shirt, untucked, along with regular old blue jeans and a pair of white sneakers. He stood on the left of Yang Haisong, who was wearing a simple, black-collared shirt, sleeves rolled up past his elbows, and slender, tight-fitting black jeans. On his right was bass guitarist Shi Xudong, who was also the drummer for the new band Guai Li. He had on a light collared, tight-fitting short-sleeved shirt and black jeans. His wispy hair had grown down to his neck and his muscular arms were covered in tattoos. Basically, he looked like a real badass, the sort of guy you didn't want to bump into on a dark night in the neighboring alley of Nanluoguxiang. In my online journal, I described him as 'a mean-looking dude—tall and thin, high cheekbones and a sallow face, with long stringy hair and a lot of energy.' Behind them was drummer Jonathan Leijonhufvud, who was originally from Sweden but had spent much of his life in China. He was thin with short, brownish hair and he looked younger than the others (at the time he was still in his 20s, and the rest of the band members were in their 30s). He wore a long-sleeved shirt with horizontal white and black stripes and no collar.

The band's neat outfits and hairdos gave them a somewhat more coherent, coordinated, and less grungy appearance than some of the other bands on the scene. Overall, they looked more mature and more well-put-together than the younger bands. The band P.K. 14 was formed in 1997 in Nanjing and moved to Beijing in 2001, where they recorded their first album, *Upstairs Turn Left*. They recorded a second album, *Whoever, Whoever, Whoever* (谁谁谁和谁谁谁) in 2004, and a third, called *White Paper* (白皮书) in 2005. Now they were busy working on a fourth album that they planned to put out on Yang Haisong and Michael Pettis's label, Maybe Mars. This was clearly a band that was dedicated and committed to their music and to their career.

The club was packed, though not quite as crowded as the tribute concerts I had witnessed there over the summer. Most of the audience members appeared to be Chinese people in their 20s. There were also plenty of foreigners in the crowd as well. Judging from their clothing and accoutrements (or lack thereof), this was a far more heterogeneous crowd than on a typical night at the smaller rock clubs 2 Kolegas or D-22. One might even qualify many of them as 'mainstream' youths, though of course the music they were listening and dancing to that night was far from what could then be considered the mainstream in China.

Yang Haisong had a husky voice. His singing came across almost like a plea, or a cry for help — with a kind of 1960s protest-era's 'Hey! Listen to what I've got to say!' feel to it. There was a slightly frantic quality to his voice, which could not really be described as melodic, at least not in the more standard sense of the word. Instead, it sounded like he was desperate to get the word out about what was going on.

That night, as Yang Haisong took center stage, the band was tight and controlled. This was not a theatrical, histrionic performance, like SUBS, Hedgehog, or Guai Li, but more of a cerebral one. The guitar, drums, and bass backed up Yang as he made his plea to the crowd. Rarely did the other band members take up any of the crowd's attention on their own. Instead, they stayed in their spots and performed. One could perceive plenty of communication going on among the band members, who were constantly turning around and looking at each other and at the drummer, like a jazz band, keeping in time and queuing each other up for the next phase of each song. Xu Bo's accompaniments, licks, riffs, and solos on guitar were restrained and methodical. Like the rail-thin singer Wen Jun of the band Guai Li, Yang Haisong stood tall, straight and stiff in the middle of the stage, not moving around too much, while holding the microphone in a tight grip. Occasionally he would let loose with a yell or a cry, raise the microphone stand, or flail his arms about, and once or twice he did a theatrical jump to end a song.

Overall, the feeling one received from watching the band was that they were supporting Yang Haisong as he told stories through his songs. For this largely Chinese audience, one big attraction of P.K. 14 was that the songs were all sung in Chinese, and the lyrics were easy to comprehend. For a Chinese person, or even a foreigner with good Chinese language skills, it was not hard to follow along and even sing along to the songs if you were familiar with them.

The band began their set with a song from their second album *Whoever...* , called 'She's Lost Her Belief' 她就失了信仰. With some simple, catchy riffs from guitarist Xu Bo, Yang Haisong chanted out the lyrics, putting a special emphasis on the phrase 'she's lost...', shouting it over and over. The final verse of the song was sung with increasing intensity as the band picked up into a crescendo, ending on 'daydreams.' A growing sense of alienation, ennui, boredom, and disillusionment seems to be the theme of this song. One detects a not-so-veiled critique of the Chinese state, which is 'on vacation' and 'getting fatter' — suggesting perhaps a country that's become flaccid and complacent and lacked spiritual values ('she's lost her belief'). While the lyrics in the album indicate that the main character in this song/story is female, the Chinese word for he/she is 'ta' which is distinguishable only in writing—so both men and women can put themselves in the place of the 'he/she' in the story. It was a unisex story after all, and one with which probably a lot of people in this audience could readily identify.

At the end of the first song, Yang Haisong told the crowd (in Mandarin), 'Hello everyone, we're P.K. 14.' There was some irony to this introduction—after all, the band was the only one playing that night and they were one of most famous bands in the Beijing scene, so it was doubtful anybody in the audience did not know who they were. There was a kind of cute politeness to the act—sort of like the Beatles introducing themselves to a London audience back in the early 1960s. And there was a Beatlesque look to the band as well, with their moppish hair, somewhat matching 'uniforms' (collared shirts, dark jeans) and their tight performances. The overall impression they left was that this was a band that knew a lot about stage presence and how to communicate with each other and with their audience. And while I may be pushing the Beatles analogy a bit too far, if I were to choose somebody from the Fab Four with whom to associate Yang Haisong, it would have to be John Lennon. They both shared a cerebral and nerdy, yet angsty and rebellious style.

Following Yang Haisong's brief introduction, the band launched into a very energetic rendition of their song '28th Shadow' (第二十八的影子). The length of the lyrical lines forced Yang Haisong to sing them out in a sort of staccato rap. The song tells the story of a dark stranger following the singer down an imaginary path, while whispering a mantra in his ear: 'This is our secret, this is our fate.' At the end of the song Yang Haisong exhorted the audience to 'turn around and let go', chanting out these words several times with increasing desperation before the song ended and the audience erupted into a frenzy of applause and cheers.

ROCKING THE CHINESE NATION

Interviews with Leading Indie Rockers: Wen Jun of Guai Li, the Members of Hedgehog, and Yang Haisong of P.K. 14

To understand better who these musicians were, where they came from, how they created their music, and what were the underlying messages and philosophies that drove their musical creations, I arranged interviews with several of these 'leading voices' of the indie rock scene in Beijing. Carried out during the fall of 2007, these interviews were largely conducted in Chinese and went in-depth for one or two hours of questioning. In this section, I offer some of the highlights of these interviews, which reveal their own personal stories as well as the attitudes of these Chinese musicians at that time towards art, music, and life in China.

Wen Jun: Lead Singer of Guai Li

In November 2007, I interviewed Wen Jun to find out more about her and her band. We conversed in Chinese in a cafe on Sanlitun North Road in the Chaoyang district of Beijing. Outside the cafe window, construction prevailed as the whole neighborhood was being rebuilt to make way for a grand new shopping mall, which would eventually host Beijing's flagship Apple store and many other icons of global capitalism. Construction workers walked back and forth on the street in thick jackets and helmets. By this time, Wen Jun had either grown out her orange hair or else had dyed it black. She was wearing a dark brown collared shirt with pink polka dots, and a thin grey sweater on top with an open neck. As we talked, I could only see her right eye, since her left eye was covered by her hair.

She told me that she came from the southern province of Guangxi, and that she first started getting interested in music in junior high school. Her primary influence was the Beatles, which she first encountered through reading the Haruki Murakami novel *Norwegian Wood* in Chinese translation (Murakami's novels are quite well known in China). She smiled like a schoolgirl and had a wistful look in her eyes, remembering those days. She explained that even though she did not understand the lyrics, she was able to sing along to the Beatles songs, and that she loved the melodies and the music. She also became interested in the 'hippy movement' that the Beatles came to represent in their later period. When I asked her if she was into Chinese music, she replied that she also loved Chinese pop music from 1930s Shanghai. She mentioned some Old Shanghai singing stars such as Bai Guang, Zhou Xuan, and Deng Lijun or Teresa Teng, the pop singer from Taiwan, who first became popular in Mainland China in the late 1970s. She told me she liked the subtleties of this old-fashioned Chinese pop music.

I asked her how she came to Beijing, and she told me that she studied for a year a technical college in Beijing and then dropped out and started playing bass for a band. This was back in 2001. Bassist He Yifan and guitarist Liu Yue, who were high school buddies, approached her to be their singer, and they got together with a drummer who lived in their compound. That was a few drummers ago. Drummers seem to come and go in these stories of band formation.

She then went on a journey to Wuhan, Chengdu, Tibet, Yunnan, and a few other remote places, returning to Beijing with another guitarist. The band was formed, and in May 2007 they started practicing and performing together. When asked why she chose the name Guai Li, she told me that the band was originally called The Dirty One, but that they changed it. She explained that it came from an ancient Chinese saying, *guai li luan shen* 怪力乱神. I later looked it up and found out that it is a line from *The Analects* (论语) attributed to the ancient sage Confucius (孔子), which scholar D.C. Lau translates as: 'The topics that the

Master did not speak of were *prodigies, force, disorder, and gods.*' In other words, Confucius did not encourage his followers to try to explain supernatural forces.

'These are strange phenomena, full of bravery. You can't use normal thinking to explain these things,' she remarked. 'Plus, I feel that *guai li* rolls off the tongue quite nicely,' she added, laughing.

When I asked Wen Jun about her method of songwriting, she told me that the band came up collectively with the tunes, and then she invented the lyrics. 'When I hear the band playing in the practice room, I just randomly sing out lyrics on the spur of the moment, subconsciously — and they aren't necessarily English; in fact, I don't usually know what language I'm singing at first. And then I go back and add lyrics that go along with the melody. It's a dialectical process, really.'

We then moved on to discuss her performance style. 'Two of my bandmates have jobs so they're often away on business,' she told me. 'So, there's often a long break in between our practice sessions. This means that when I perform songs, I'm usually performing the same ones over and over, since we don't have the time to practice new ones. A lot of bands have this problem.' I asked her if this impedes her ability to create new songs. She shrugged and responded:

> I don't create a lot of new songs; I just sing the same ones over again. That's bad, but on the other hand I feel that every time I perform, there's a different feeling to the songs. But it's hard to tell what sort of feeling it will be at first; sometimes you're happy and other times angry and so on. You can always keep finding new feelings and new positions in the same song.

ANDREW DAVID FIELD

Zi Jian (l), Atom (m), and Bo Xuan (r) during an interview with the author in 2007 (video still by Andrew Field)

Z.O., BoX, and Atom of Hedgehog

After their concert at D-22 in August 2007, the band members of Hedgehog also agreed to do an interview with me, which eventually took place later that fall in their practice room downtown. On a Tuesday night, I headed over to the Wangfujing district, where I found their practice room in a subterranean parking lot under a big office building. There were two adjoining rooms, one leading into another. The first room was full of guitars and amps and the walls were covered with posters of record albums, some of them classic and others recently released by Beijing indie bands. Clearly this was a practice space that supported many different bands from the local indie music scene. In the inner room, a much smaller room lined with sound proofing on the walls and a big mirror on one end, the members of Hedgehog were busy setting up their instruments. They stopped playing and got seated on a couch for the interview, with Atom in the middle flanked by Z.O. on her right and BoX on her left. We conversed in Mandarin as I shot them question after question.

They told me that they grew up in Beijing, and that they met in junior year of high school. The band Hedgehog was originally just Z.O. and BoX. Atom joined later. They had been playing together for three years. Z.O. said that he had not had any formal training in music. Neither had the others. 'We're just rank amateurs,' admitted Atom. When I asked them how they learned music, they smiled and exchanged glances with each other.

'I started out by buying a book of folk music, with diagrams of the simple chords, you know, C, F, and the like,' said Z.O. 'And then I'd listen to CDs and study the songs, and slowly I picked them up.' BoX told a similar story, about how he learned music from CDs and books, and from a friend who taught him some chords.

What attracted them to rock music? 'I just found that rock music moved me in a way that other music didn't,' shrugged BoX, as Atom giggled. 'It was just more interesting.'

'Actually, there are some things,' picked up Atom, 'that you don't know why you like them, but you just can't leave them alone. It's like being lovestruck or something — like when you fall in love with somebody, but you don't know why.'

The testimony of the band reflected the prevailing attitude in the indie scene that authenticity was a key part of the scene.

'I think that rock'n'roll is part of youth culture,' added Z.O. 'At base it's an impetuous, genuine feeling, without any affectations — an unaffected kind of music. At least the kind of rock music that really attracts me is the more direct, primitive kind.'

Atom then took back the mic. 'I think that rock music is like a mirror,' she mused. 'It reflects who you really are inside. Some people seem totally fake [on stage], while others seem genuine — it comes from inside of you.'

As for BoX: 'It's all about freedom; it's a truer kind of

Yang Haisong during an interview with the author in 2007 (video still by Andrew Field)

performance. Rock music came to China from the West, and it hasn't had that much of a history here, but now it's starting to take on Chinese characteristics.'

Genuine and with Chinese characteristics—these qualities seemed to be what these bands valued most about their music and their identities as rock musicians in China.

Yang Haisong: Lead Singer of PK-14

After I saw him in concert in November 2007, I arranged to meet and interview Yang Haisong. On a very cold day in December, we were sitting in a cafe in Sanlitun, the same one where I interviewed Guai Li's lead singer Wen Jun. He leaned back in a plush red high-backed sofa that looked like it was designed for royalty—and in a way, he *was* royalty, at least in the indie music scene. 'Oh, there's another life you can live,' he told me in emphatic tones. 'It's a different life. You must very very serious to your life.'

Yang Haisong wore his hair in a somewhat short yet vaguely Beatlesque mop on his head. Feathery bangs hung over his forehead, and hair covered his ears and the back of his neck.

ROCKING THE CHINESE NATION

He was tall and lean, with wizened eyes that looked beyond his age (he was 33 years old that year). He sported a pair of thick eyeglasses, frameless around the lenses except for the dark red frame holding them on top. His glasses looked to be knockoffs of the classic and trendy Ray-Ban Clubmasters. On the day of the interview, he wore a thin black knit sweater with a brown shirt collar sticking out of the V-neck. He smoked cigarettes as he spoke in an animated fashion, with plenty of laughing and grinning and wide hand gestures, and with eyes that sparkled with intelligence and lit up as he told me his stories. He had thick lips and a wide face with quizzical brows. Overall, he gave off the radiance of a man of intellect, and a person who thought very carefully about both his appearance and his words.

Yang Haisong told me he first took an interest in rock music while growing up in the southern city of Nanjing, a former imperial capital of China in the early Ming dynasty, again the national capital in the 1930s, and now the capital city of Jiangsu Province. With a population of 6.5 million, it is the second largest city in eastern China, next to Shanghai. As Yang Haisong reminded me, Nanjing has always been well-known as an intellectual and cultural capital, with a large concentration of universities, historic sites including Sun Yat-sen's Mausoleum and museums. Many great novelists and poets came from this city. Yang Haisong himself came from a family of intellectuals. His mother was a lawyer and a teacher of 'culture'. His father, he said, was a 'serious man'.

The first band to attract Yang Haisong to rock music was the Chinese metal band Tang Dynasty. Listening to the band in 1993 on a radio show in Nanjing gave him the idea that 'there's another life you can live.' He described the experience to me in English: 'The music is quite weird, you know, very noisy, and very powerful. Actually, it scared me, scared me a lot.' He told me that he borrowed a cassette tape of the first album of Tang Dynasty from a friend. Reading the lyrics of the songs gave him another idea: It's okay to rebel. If there is a message to the music, he said, it is this: 'It's not like I do what they want, my parents or my teacher, or all the society, all the mainstream want me to be. I don't want to be what they want. I want to be me. I want to be myself, and I should think of myself, my life, and…life is myself,' he laughed. 'It's a message in the lyrics, and it was really inspiring me.' He was speaking of the lyrics of the Tang Dynasty songs. What or whom was he rebelling against? What else, but parents and school?

'Actually, I quit the university.' This was back in 1993, when he was attending school in Nanjing. He told me that he was training to be an engineer, but that he quit from lack of interest. 'When I quit, I wanted to be a novelist or poet. I wanted to write something, to be a writer. And one day I thought, oh yeah, maybe I can become a musician, and I can play drums or something. And then I learned to play drums and play guitars and write songs myself.' He confessed that he loved to read novels and poems, and that he wanted to be a poet. Thus, he dropped out of school and took up music instead.

'How did your family feel about your decision to quit engineering and study music?' I asked.

'Very angry,' he answered, shaking his head and grinning. 'Very upset. Very, very upset. But now it's okay, now they understand what I think. But at that time, there was a lot of arguing, a lot of screaming. I think it was very hard for them at that time. Even harder than for me.'

Yang Haisong's story is a reminder of the sacrifices that he and so many others in the Chinese indie rock scene were making to play their music. They had given up on the more well-trodden career paths, dropped out of school, compromised their relations with their parents and families, forsaken the dream of owning a home and a car, and in some cases, of even getting married and having children. Instead, they devoted their lives to making music, in a city and country in which making music—at least the indie music they loved—did not lead to fame or fortune. As Michael Pettis testified:

> If you go to New York or London, three quarters of the people in the music scene are doing it because they don't know what else to do or because it's sort of cool, or because you get to dress funny or whatever. Here [in China] it's not like that; if you're in the music scene, you're damn serious about music, because it's not like a cool alternative. You give up your place on the treadmill, the job treadmill, you're not getting back on again. And you're going to be harassed by your parents on a daily basis, it's just really not easy.

Yang Haisong was something of an enigma. He was one of the most articulate people in the Chinese indie music scene, and he had emerged as one of the scene's leading voices. In addition to being a singer and songwriter, he was also an artist, a music producer, and a poet. Like a Chinese Pied Piper, or perhaps China's own Buddy Holly or John Lennon—a nerdy, glasses-wearing everyman, who conquered and seduced the world with his charms and his songs—he and his band P.K. 14 were leading a whole new generation of youth in China to drop whatever else they were doing, pick up instruments, write songs, and start bands of their own.

Where did Yang Haisong get his poetic tendencies, and who were his biggest influences? He replied that his first and foremost influence was his mother. 'My mother is a teacher of language and culture,' he explained. 'So, actually, she can understand a lot. But my father, he is a very serious person. Very, very serious. You know, it's hard to see him smile or laugh. He's very serious. So, yeah. I think it's harder for them than me for this decision.'

He was referring of course to his decision to get off the standard Chinese career path of being an engineer and become a poet and a musician. Apparently, Yang Haisong inherited his creative genes from his mother and his discipline and hardworking nature from his father. Both these sets of traits had prepared him well for a life as a singer, song writer, and musician in the Chinese indie scene.

He then told me more about his musical and literary influences.

'I like to sing. I like to write songs,' he said, adding that among his biggest influences were Phil Ochs, Bob Dylan, and Woody Guthrie. I was used to hearing about Nirvana, The Ramones, or The Clash as influences, so I was taken aback to hear the names of the great troubadours of folk and folk-rock music in American culture. He also threw in Neil Young for good measure: 'I think a whole generation of protest music, I think it influenced me, not only the music, but the world view.' Among the tunes he admired was Bob Dylan's classic song 'Ballad of a Thin Man,' with the indubitable Mr. Jones. 'I think it's the best song to express how to face the change in those days. And I think now it's the same situation. We should understand how to face the change in the new China. Nowadays, China is changing a lot. So I think it's the same situation.' In terms of his literary influences, Yang Haisong was into the Beat Generation authors. He mentioned the writers Allen Ginsberg, Jack Kerouac, and William S. Burroughs.

'In my opinion, there are two Chinas,' he told me in a mixture of Chinese and English. 'One is the China that we see: all of the prosperity, the modernity. As in New York, Tokyo, Berlin, or

Paris. You can see this in Beijing. You can see all the modernity, all of the people's lives, and you can say this is modern China. Everything's fine. Everything's okay.'

As he spoke, I looked out over the Sanlitun area, which was rapidly morphing from a grungy expat-oriented bar street in the heart of the embassy district of Beijing into an ultramodern commercial district full of high rises and shopping malls.

'But in my life, you can also see that there's another China. Some people's lives are not the same. They are quite young. They live in small towns, middle cities or something. Nothing's interesting, and they have to face the tough situations, for living, only for living.'

These were the kids you saw when traveling just about anywhere in China outside of the main cities like Beijing and Shanghai. As for the nation's youth:

"They have energy, but they don't know how to be creative. They have more energy, but I think it's tough for them. Actually, I wrote this song for the young. I hope there's a message, very simple, and they just register it, for the young people. They have a passion, but the passion has just no direction. They don't know how to express their energy. They want to do something, but they don't know why they should do this."

We now seemed to be heading into political territory. After the ominous events of 1989, staging public protests of an overtly political nature became both difficult and dangerous in China. Yang Haisong and his musician and artist friends were aware of this unstated line, and they tend to avoid any direct confrontation with the ideologies and policies of the Party, preferring as did the poets of old to clothe their protests in subtler garb. One could argue that rock music is not a subtle form of art, but there is a huge difference between singing the poetic lyrics of P.K. 14's songs, and shouting out 'God Save the Queen of the fascist regime that made you a moron,' as the Sex Pistols did, or any of the other in-your-face-and-up-yours lyrics of the punk and hardcore movements in the U.K. and America, not to mention the folk musicians who preceded them, and the rappers who followed.

'But China's a little subtler,' I offered as he plunged into a discussion on politics.

'Yes, I can understand,' he responded. 'Actually, even for young Chinese, it's also confusing. It's very complex, about the right and the left. You know, in theory, China is a communist country, so we should be leftist, but now we have embraced capitalism. It's also quite confusing for the Chinese, even for me.'

I asked him if he saw rock in China as a political movement and he quickly became defensive: 'I don't want to talk politics. We are not a political band. For me, I might not want to be a politician, and I don't want to talk about it.' But after that, he pondered for a moment and admitted: 'For me, everything is involved with politics. So you cannot run away from that, you have to face it. For me, it's a protest song for them. For the young generation, for the new people.'

While the lyrics of some of his songs might have a subtle political strain to them, the power lies in the music itself. Going back to the concert at MAO Live House on a chilly November night, aside from a few die-hard fans who took the time to read the lyrics sheet in their CDs, it's likely that most of the audience members weren't that familiar with the lyrical content of the songs. Instead, they were there to see the show and take in the visceral sounds and rhythms of one of China's premier indie rock bands.

'Yeah, we like to have more power and energy on the stage,' said Yang Haisong during my interview with him. 'We like to send a message to the audience. More power. For me, we are a rock and roll band, not only post-punk. We have some roots from post-punk, but now it's rock. Rock and roll.'

As the scene's most prominent poet and statesman, Yang defended the importance of his lyrics: 'For me, the lyrics are the most important thing. In rock and roll music, the amazing part of it is the lyrics.'

From their onstage personae and their offstage conversations, it was clear that Wen Jun of Guai Li, the three band members of Hedgehog, and Yang Haisong of P.K.-14 were rebels with a cause. They were working hard to push the envelope of indie music in China, drawing from a wide pool of influences ranging from beat poets to folk artists to rock musicians from the western world, as well as influential bands in China such as Tang Dynasty. In carving out a life for themselves as musicians in the indie rock scene, they had sacrificed more conventional pathways, forgone more lucrative careers, and weathered the anger of their parents. These brave artists were forging a new music for China and were sending out powerful if sometimes mysterious messages to a small yet loyal audience. Who could tell at the time that over the next decade or more, their voices would reach millions of Chinese youths as the market for indie music in China expanded through the power of social media? As I discuss in a later chapter, their music and their messages also resonated with the band SUBS and its charismatic lead singer Kang Mao, whom I also interviewed in the summer of 2007 and again over many years of following the band. They also harmonized with some of the ideas and philosophies of China's rock godfather, Cui Jian. Meanwhile, their music and its messages were being vigorously promoted by a loyal cadre of music promoters, concert and festival organizers, and record producers, who together with the bands and their fans completed the circle of the Chinese indie music scene. It is to these people we turn next.

3

BRINGING INDIE MUSIC TO A WIDER AUDIENCE IN CHINA: EVENT PROMOTERS, RECORD LABELS, AND ROCK FESTIVALS

WHILE THE CLUBS of Beijing were nurturing new bands and sounds in the city's indie scene, other people were helping those bands to reach a wider audience by producing their record albums and holding special events and festivals to showcase them. One of the supporters of China's indie rock scene was Lao Yang, owner of one of China's leading independent music record shops. Through Lao Yang, I learned a great deal about independent music in China as well as some of the challenges of music distribution. Lao Yang supported many of the bands that were on the way to stardom in the scene, such as Carsick Cars. He also favored and supported the more experimental side of China's music scenes. One example is Carsick Cars front man Zhang Shouwang, whom Lao Yang was encouraging to stretch by offering his shop as a venue for performances of a more experimental nature. Another was a weekly music event held at 2 Kolegas which Lao Yang attended and supported, known as Waterland Kwanyin.

Meanwhile, across the city, Michael Pettis was on the way to becoming a driving force behind the elevation of many bands in China's indie rock scene towards national and international stardom, or at least recognition. The seminal year 2007 saw the formation of his new record label, Maybe Mars Records. This new label was started by Michael and his partner Yang Haisong, to represent new bands and more experimental currents in the rock scenes in Beijing and elsewhere in China. A counterpart to Maybe Mars was Matt Kagler's indie label, Tag Team Records. With their marquee band Lonely China Day and a few other bands on their label, Tag Team Records was struggling to survive in the music industry in both China and abroad. In an interview I did with him late in 2007, Matt discussed the trials and tribulations of indie music record making and distribution in China and revealed his own philosophy and attitudes towards music and life.

At the same time, music festivals, usually held outdoors in large spaces such as public parks, were introducing rock music and the local indie scene to a much wider and more diverse audience. These included the MIDI Festival, the Beijing Pop Festival, and the Modern Sky Festival. These festivals, all of which took place in 2007, showcased local Beijing rock bands while also providing a much larger audience with exposure to dozens of major rock acts and pop bands coming to China from the outside world to perform their music.

The 798 Art Zone and the Crossovers between Art, Music, and Commerce

Located in Chaoyang District beyond the 4th Ring Road, the 798 Art Zone was the leading arts district in the city of Beijing. In the leadup to the 2008 Olympics, the district was already earning a reputation as the world's largest showcase of contemporary Chinese artists and their works. It arose out of a neighborhood composed of red brick and gray concrete factories in a landscape punctuated by tall smokestacks. The district was dominated by a Bauhaus-style munitions factory (no. 798) constructed for the

Manager Liu Kai playing guitar on the front steps of the Sugar Jar Record Shop in 798 Arts District in summer 2007 (photo by Andrew Field)

Chinese by the East Germans in the 1950s. This and many other former state-owned factories and warehouses in the district came to serve as art galleries, interspersed with cafes, restaurants, bookstores, and shops.

Among the dozens of establishments in the 798 Art Zone was a record shop called Sugar Jar (白糖罐). Its founder was a tall, reedy man with a goatee named Lao Yang. He came from the Northeast region of China and had been deeply involved in the avant-garde art and music scenes in Beijing for many years. Lao Yang was a veritable encyclopedia of independent music and arts in China, and he supported the scene through special events held in his record shop. I first met Lao Yang at a party held in July 2007 in one of the signature galleries in the district, the Times Space Gallery (时代空间). This gallery was built out of the former munitions factory—you could even see the German labeling on some of the original fixtures in the main hallway leading to the gallery, and the Bauhaus-style wave-like ceiling of the gallery features revolutionary slogans painted during the Mao era stating: 'Long live Chairman Mao, our Great Helmsman'. Such Cultural Revolution era slogans served as an ironic counterpoint to the events and exhibitions going on below them.

Sponsored by Tiger Beer, the party held that evening in the factory-turned-gallery space featured several art performances and live music acts. Six graffiti artists from several different countries, including China and Australia, worked on huge canvases lining the walls of the gallery, and they also painted graffiti art on several white couches. A Chinese woman in a swimsuit performed a dance while immersed in a tank of water, which drew a huge crowd of onlookers. Accompanying her dance was a musician playing electronic music from a laptop. It turned out that the musician was Dou Wei, founding member of Black Panther 黑豹. Later, Helen Feng, the singer for the band

Ziyo 自游, made an appearance as well and rocked the crowd with a set with her other band, Nova Heart.

Lubricated by copious amounts of Tiger Beer, the event reinforced the connections between avant-garde music and art. Like the famous Mudd Club in downtown Manhattan, where artists such as Keith Haring and Jean-Michel Basquiat once showcased their works, 798 Art Zone provided a platform for artists and musicians to get together, share ideas, and combine their performances. This sponsored event also underscored the relentless forces of commercialization that turn art and music into commodities for sale on the global market. The 798 Art Zone itself was a conduit for the manifestation of this process. Over the first few years of its development, most of the original founding artists had been pushed out of the Art Zone as rents climbed and fancy shops and galleries took the place of artists' studios.

An Interview with Lao Yang, owner of Sugar Jar Record Shop
In the summer and fall of 2007, I paid several visits to the 798 Art Zone and I always stopped in at the Sugar Jar. The Sugar

Lao Yang, owner of Sugar Jar Record Shop in 798 Arts District, at the entrance to his shop in 2007. The Chinese name for the shop is on the chalk board (video still by Andrew Field)

ROCKING THE CHINESE NATION

Jar was a small shop with one of its walls lined floor-to-ceiling with CDs of independent music. Among the offerings were not just rock music CDs, but also electronica and other genres of independent music. It was without doubt the largest single collection of Chinese independent music assembled anywhere. The ever-friendly Lao Yang was a copious source of information, and he offered me plenty of recommendations for bands to listen to and follow. Based on his recommendations, I assembled my own collection of Chinese independent music CDs. Some of them were veteran rock acts, while others were just beginning to emerge as the darlings of the Beijing indie rock scene.

While Lao Yang came and went from the shop, the manager in charge of the Sugar Jar was a young musician named Liu Kai. He also proved to be a very helpful source of information on indie music, not just in China but worldwide. He continually downloaded digital music, underscoring the importance of the internet and mp3s to the spread of musical knowledge in China, and he played songs by many different bands on the shop's stereo system. Over the summer and fall I learned a great deal from Liu Kai about global trends in indie music.

In November 2007, I conducted an interview with Lao Yang. He told me that the Sugar Jar began as a tiny shop outside the gates of Tsinghua University back in 2003, and he moved the shop to the 798 Art Zone in October 2005. When I asked him why he chose 798 as his new location, he had an immediate response: 'Because 798 is the most active stage for contemporary arts culture in China, and this is pretty much the most vibrant and provocative [cultural] site in all of China. I chose 798 because it's a really great stage for promoting indie rock music in China.' We continued to talk about the development of indie rock in China and he described the stages of its development from the early 'youthful' years of the 1990s, when musicians in China were imitating any rock music they could find from the western world, to the current stage of development, where musicians in China were now creating their own original sounds and moving into the global arena of independent music.

We then switched to the topic of record companies. With a slightly perceptible scowl, he related his own disdain for the recorded music industry, an ironic gesture from the man who ran the most comprehensive independent music record shop in all of China: 'I reckon that record companies can't really have a very direct relationship with independent music. And that's because record companies are all about making money—that's their main goal. When choosing music, they don't really care about what kind of music you are making, but rather whether they can make a profit off of it.' He looked around at his own collection on the walls of his shop and added, 'These albums here, you will only see them very rarely in other record shops in China.'

True enough—one would be hard pressed to find almost any of the albums in Lao Yang's Sugar Jar at a more conventional store in China selling CDs, even though more 'mainstream' western pop-rock bands from the Rolling Stones to Coldplay could be found in most of such stores at the time.

In addition to discussing the rise and fall of various indie record labels in China, Lao Yang shared with me a list of bands that he found more compelling from the indie rock scene. These bands include names like Glorious Pharmacy (美好药店), Top Floor Circus (顶楼的马戏团), and Mafeisan, some of which have put out their own independent labels to produce indie music. He told me that his favorite rock-folk artist was Zuoxiao Zuzhou 左小祖咒, who rarely performed concerts. There were also bands in his list of favorites going back to the 1990s, like Tongue (舌头) and The Fly (苍蝇) and some others that he recommended listening to, which produced some very bizarre and scatological music—I would hesitate to call it unlistenable, but certainly not having any real commercial value. Some of these bands reminded me of avant-garde, experimental fringe bands like Snakefinger and the Residents, and other artists on the enigmatic indie label Ralph Records, which I listened to as a teenager.

As we discussed the process of making independent records, Lao Yang reminded me that there were certain restrictions to making and distributing indie record albums in China. 'If you want to make demos of your music, that's one thing,' he told me. 'If you want to sell them that's another matter entirely, and you have to go through a review process by the national government's Ministry of Culture, and if you haven't gone through this process of review, it's illegal to sell your records.'

To go through this process, he added, you had to be producing your record with a licensed record company. Also, there was a lower limit to the number of copies that could be produced legally, so if you were only producing dozens or even hundreds of albums, it was still illegal to do so. In other words, the law greatly limited the legal ability of independent artists in China to distribute and sell their recorded works.

When I asked him what common traits existed among the younger Chinese indie bands that he favored, which at the time included P.K. 14, SUBS, Hedgehog, and Carsick Cars, he went into a rather lengthy discourse about the nature of independent music, the rock'n'roll spirit, and what makes certain bands worth following:

> It's really about a thought process, this notion of 'independence'. Rock music (摇滚) originally came to China from the western world. And for China's youths, the first step towards independence was listening to rock'n'roll. Rock'n'roll music represents a rock'n'roll

spirit, and in China it was through the perspective of this spirit that our understanding of rock music first developed. And so-called rock'n'roll spirit has a lot of rebelliousness, at least in its outward appearance. Yet this sort of rebellion isn't necessarily the product of a process of deep thought, but rather a natural and instinctive bodily reaction [to the music]. Every young person in the bloom of youth will naturally have a disposition towards rebellion, and this rebellious disposition won't necessarily transform itself into an independent spirit. Many people rebel in their youth, but then step right into the social structure that they were previously opposing and become an element of that society and stand on the opposite side to what they were rebelling against as youths. Therefore, what I recognize as independent rock music, aside from studying western rock music and its methods of expression and building its own creative style, it's also about the thought [the musicians] apply to their own lives and about taking a creative pathway that blends western rock music with musical traditions from China to create something new that isn't just imitating others but that is both original and localized. It comes out of thinking about one's own cultural environment and producing something that relates to that. At least this for me is the entry point for considering bands in the indie rock scene that are worth paying attention to.

Lao Yang emphasized that the Sugar Jar not only served as a space for selling indie record albums that were extremely difficult to find otherwise, but it also functioned as a center for the promotion of independent music of many different types and genres. In addition, he maintained an archive for materials relating to independent music and had an online music radio station that Liu Kai operated (no wonder he had such great knowledge of indie rock—he was a radio DJ). Every Sunday they hosted special events and live performance by local artists. One that I attended featured Carsick Cars front man, Zhang Shouwang.

An Experimental Performance by Zhang Shouwang and Simon Frank at Sugar Jar (11 Nov 2007)

On a cold Sunday in November, I visited the Sugar Jar in 798 to observe Zhang Shouwang giving an experimental performance. He was joined by a handsome, curly-headed Canadian teenager named Simon Frank. Simon played an electronic keyboard as Shouwang conducted what might be called scientific experiments with his guitar in front of an intimate gathering of friends and fans. He used various implements to apply pressure to or strum the strings of his guitar, including a violin bow, a pressure tool, and a slider. The result was not very musical in the conventional sense. Like the performers in the Waterland Kwanyin series at 2 Kolegas that Lao Yang also supported along with its founder Yan Jun, Zhang Shouwang and Simon Frank were experimenting and pushing the envelope of what constitutes music, just as avant-garde artists continually push the boundaries of what constitutes art.

After their performance, I talked with Shouwang and Simon in the Galleria Continua, an art gallery located across the alleyway from the Sugar Jar. The gallery was featuring an exhibition by Indian artist Anish Kapoor, in which a spiral tunnel led into a central chamber of this chimney-topped-warehouse-turned-gallery space, where a large vacuum tube sucked vaporized water from the floor up to the high ceiling, creating a sculpture of vapor. Amidst installations of big shiny chrome-colored balls, Shouwang and Simon briefly explained the scene to me.

'What's so interesting about the music scene in Beijing?' I asked.

> Shouwang: Lots of new bands just came out at the same time, and they're doing quite interesting stuff. Everyone works together. So the small music scene can create lots of new stuff.
>
> Simon: What's so great is that it's pretty small, small enough so that there's like a close-knit community. The bands are really diverse. You have everything from garage punk to like post-punk and more noisy stuff like this.
>
> Shouwang: That's what's great about Beijing, because there are a lot of musicians or artists who have a lot of freedom to do their own stuff. But in London or New York it's not like that anymore...because other clubs try to make money. There's actually no money for the music scene in Beijing...
>
> Simon: Since the music scene hasn't been around that long it hasn't really fallen into established patterns, so every now and then something can like peek up that is really weird, and you wouldn't see elsewhere. There still are a lot of people who are just in it for the music, you could say like D-22, the people at Dos Kolegas and Sugar Jar where we just played.

Despite or perhaps because of their youth, the pair shared surprisingly keen insights into the dynamism and uniqueness of the Beijing indie scene. Shouwang and Simon both emphasized its lack of commercialism, as well as its newness and the relative freedom of musicians to experiment with new sounds and styles, which they had just exemplified through their intimate performance at the Sugar Jar.

More Experimentation: Waterland Kwanyin at 2 Kolegas
Lao Yang seemed to be drawn to more avant-garde music and performance culture, which was truly independent of any commercial drives. Another scene he supported was an experimental music night at 2 Kolegas organized by a local artist named Yan Jun. Named after the mythical paradise inhabited by the Buddhist Goddess of Mercy, known as Waterland Kwanyin (水路观音), the event took place every Tuesday night, and Lao Yang encouraged me to check it out. Over the summer and fall of 2007, I attended several performances. The first was by a Japanese man, who performed straight from his laptop. The sounds that emerged, amplified by the club speakers, sounded more like the engine of a jet plane than music. Lao Yang was there that night and he seemed to be greatly enjoying this act, which definitely pushed the concept of 'music' to its limits and beyond.

Stretching the limits of what constitutes music was an important part of the music scene that was unfolding in Beijing, and Lao Yang was very supportive of this trend. At events such as Waterland Kuanyin, which Lao Yang frequented (I met him there during other visits to the event later that year), the boundary lines between music and pure noise were constantly being stretched and challenged, as they always had been in the history of rock and roll. On another evening, November 28 to be precise, I headed over to 2 Kolegas to catch a performance featuring a young Danish man kneeling on the stage surrounded by various instruments and pieces of equipment, including a mandolin, three brass bowls, and a number of distortion pedals jacked up to the system, and watched as he created 'music' by running a violin bow across the bowls and mandolin and tapping them with a screwdriver. The results were eerie, and the sound was like that of a high-pitched saw blade slicing into one's brain. The sounds of this performance were familiar to any apartment resident in China who has had to put up with the noise of neighboring apartments undergoing renovations, though in a much higher register.

Two other young European artists then mounted the stage, and using a laptop computer, they create sounds not too dissimilar to the Japanese fellow earlier that summer, like those of a jet-plane refueling. Put together with the previous performance, it could be viewed as a perfect evocation of the noisy construction environment of China, or anywhere in the world developing fast for that matter. An audience of around twenty people, a quite young mix of foreigners and some curious Chinese youths, watched this performance intently, though not without some looks of skepticism. Was this music? Sound? Noise? What was the purpose of this performance, if not to stretch our understanding of music itself?

The Formation of the Maybe Mars Record Label

One of the most important developments in Chinese indie music was the birth of a new record label known as Maybe Mars 兵马司. The label was created in the fall of 2007 by Yang Haisong and Michael Pettis. Until they started their new label, options for bands releasing albums on local labels had been limited. As Yang Haisong explained, 'There were only maybe one or two labels, Modern Sky or Scream. A lot of bands have no choice, they just maybe play music for one or two years, then break up. Maybe they have talent, maybe they have creativity, but they stop playing, which I think is a great shame for the industry.' Michael Pettis also related the story of how and why he and

ROCKING THE CHINESE NATION

Yang Haisong got together to form the new label to encourage the bands they were promoting at D-22 to make albums:

> Because we've been so supportive of the scene, our club is where all the musicians hang out. They get free drinks, so of course they hang out there. A lot of them think of the club D-22 as sort of like the home base of the Beijing music scene, and we've been getting a lot of requests for a while. You know, 'Why don't you guys put out a CD label?' I had been resisting it. It's a lot of work and the club alone is enough work. Plus I have my day job where I make the money that I lose on the club. For a long time we thought maybe one day we'll do it. Finally, we decided, let's just start our own label, because for some of these bands, we really need to produce high-quality records. We started the label Maybe Mars. I asked Yang Haisong if he would run it, and he had been dying to do something like that for years. We put the label together, and immediately released the Carsick Cars CD, which Yang Haisong produced, and the Snapline CD, which Martin Atkins, the former drummer of Public Image, produced, and Joyside, one of the older bands that we like a great deal. They're one of the most famous bands of the older generation. We put out those three CDs, and things started going really well. We had a lot of attention, they were selling quite quickly in China within the indie scene, and we realized that we really have something exciting going here.

Over the next two decades, Yang Haisong and the Maybe Mars label would go on to produce and disseminate record albums by dozens of indie rock bands that were at the 'cutting edge' of the indie music scene in China. This new label was also a kind of rebellion against the bigger labels, including the Beijing label Modern Sky, which were moving towards more of a commercial model, seeking to simply profit from the bands they represented rather than encouraging them to play highly original music that pushed the boundaries of rock and of music in general. By backing bands that had no obvious commercial potential, and whose music was experimental, noisy, and edgy, the founders of Maybe Mars were making a statement about authenticity shared by many others whom I encountered in Chinese rock scenes.

The Maybe Mars Album Release Party at the New Yugong Yishan (10 November 2007)
To celebrate the founding of their new label, Michael Pettis and Yang Haisong organized a release party featuring performances by some of the bands whose records they produced along with others they were supporting and nourishing. The concert took place at the new Yugong Yishan rock club. The club had moved from the Worker's Stadium/Sanlitun area in eastern Beijing to a more central location on Zhangzizhong Road, right next to the former headquarters of Republican China President, Duan Qirui. He was in power during the famed May Fourth Movement of 1919, when thousands of university students gathered at Tiananmen to protest the Duan government's signing of the Treaty of Versailles, which handed over territory in Shandong Province formerly occupied by Germans to the Japanese. Now, nearly ninety years later, Chinese university students were moving to the rhythms of rock and roll as they entered the club next door.

The premises of the club were fronted with old Beijing bricks. A large, imposing red door served as the main entrance. A sign with the Chinese characters 愚公移山 was prominently displayed vertically on a lit-up sign box outside the door, and below the name was a figure of a man raising a large pickaxe over his head and readying it for a blow. The cavernous club could hold over 600 people and it featured a much more high-end sound system than the previous club venue. After entering an entrance hall, where one could purchase tickets and check one's coat, one then walked up into an elevated bar area featuring a large square bar where bartenders were serving drinks to the customers. Surrounding the bar were some small tables where customers could hang out. Beyond the bar were stairs leading down into the main open pit area in front of the stage, which could hold several hundred people. In all the concerts I saw there, the audience tended to cluster tightly near the stage, which was elevated much higher than the stages at other rock clubs in the city. Basically, from the audience space right in front of the stage, one was looking up at the feet of the band members playing above one's head.

That evening, one of the bands on the new Maybe Mars label called Snapline performed a set of strange and hypnotic tunes, which reminded me of some of the more avant-garde punk rock bands I used to listen to in high school. Their music could have been featured in a David Lynch film. The band was fronted by tall, thin singer, Chen Xi, who was dressed like a hipster from the 1950s, and whose physical appearance and style reminded me of Yang Haisong (so much that I mistook Yang for Chen at one point during the night). The post-punk band Guai Li also performed that evening, as did Hedgehog, joyously playing their 'noisepop' tunes to the crowd. These bands did their best to fill the large space of this new rock club and do justice to its much bigger stage. Carsick Cars stole the show that night with riveting performances by Zhang Shouwang and his bandmates. Behind the band, the Maybe Mars sign was prominently displayed in the middle of the stage, showcasing the new label that produced their first album.

During the height of the event, the crowd went wild to the Carsick Cars tune 'Zhongnanhai'. This song is either a paean to a famous cigarette brand in China, or else a not-too-subtle reference to the area of the Forbidden City, where the country's current leadership resides. This is the band's most identifiable song, and it was easy for the audience to sing along. As usual, Zhang Shouwang performed an energetic guitar solo, giving it a distinctive post-industrial sound as he striated the strings rapidly up and down the fret board.

The marquee band's performance, as well as those of the other bands on the Maybe Mars label, or soon to be on the label, was a fitting celebration of a new indie record label that would go on over the next several years to produce albums by dozens of avant-garde indie rock bands in China. Carsick Cars would go on to make a name for themselves on the international indie music circuit.

Zhang Shouwang performing with his band Carsick Cars at the Maybe Mars Record Label launch party at Yugong Yishan on 10 Nov 2007 (photo by Andrew Field)

ROCKING THE CHINESE NATION

Cynical Views: An Interview with Tag Team Records Owner Matt Kagler

Maybe Mars co-founders Pettis and Yang embodied an optimistic can-do attitude about the future of indie rock music in China. Matt Kagler on the other hand was somewhat skeptical, if not downright cynical about the future of rock music in China and of his own label, Tag Team Records. He operated his label out of a small office in the Houhai Lake area in the middle of the city. Tag Team Records had already produced albums for a handful of bands including Lonely China Day, Arrows Made of Desire, and a band from Athens, Georgia called Venice is Sinking. The label was clearly struggling to keep its head above water and had even collaborated with the larger indie record company Modern Sky to internationally distribute an EP by a well-known Chinese indie band called Rebuilding the Rights of Statues or Re-TROS, which I saw perform in Shanghai that summer during the Rock It Festival (I describe both the festival and the band later in the book).

During the fall of 2007, I talked with Matt Kagler at a cafe in the Nanluoguxiang alleyway near his home and office. Nanluoguxiang is nestled in a warren of *hutong* alleyways, old Beijing neighborhoods with courtyard homes known as *siheyuan* 四合院, some of which used to house Manchu noblemen and Chinese generals back in the days of the Qing Dynasty. Like all the other areas that surround Houhai, Nanluoguxiang was rapidly in process of becoming a commercialized strip of cafes, restaurants, boutique shops and hotels catering to Chinese and international tourists, which ironically was probably the only way to save this centuries-old neighborhood from demolition.

While quaffing a Qingdao beer and puffing on cigarettes, Matt related the story of founding his label, which began with his discovery of Lonely China Day. 'In a nutshell, I was living in Beijing, I had some previous experience working in the music industry in the US, and I think I had a nice comfortable life in China. Then all of a sudden I saw this band one night, and I thought, these guys are really amazing.' He stopped to take a swig of beer, scratched his long red beard, and continued: 'I mean they really represent the best of both East and the West, and they're a band called Lonely China Day. It was a huge breath of fresh air to see a band that was unique.'

When I asked Matt how he would describe an LCD show, he replied: 'I think that Lonely China Day play music for people with big souls. They're certainly not making light music; it's not something you're really going to bounce around to.' Like other observers, in his talk of the 'soul' he was averring to something spiritual about the music, with its oceanic qualities. 'But then again,' he added, 'they do have a live show, they do put on a show. It's a heavy thing, but not in a heavy sort of rock kind of way. It can get that way. It ebbs and flows. I think it's very organic music they make, and I think their stage show really reflects that.' His observations squared with what I witnessed at CH+INDIE Fest and at other LCD concerts I saw previously that summer.

Matt then continued with his story of the founding of Tag Team Records:

> We thought we could really do something with these guys, and so we made a few phone calls. I called my brother who was working with Rhino [Records] at the time, and thought let's release a record, let's do it on a limited edition basis, but let's put it out in the States, and so we got to talking with the band, and they said let's put the record out in China first, and then let's put it out in the States.

Thus, inspired by an LCD performance, and with the aid of some Beijing-based friends, Tag Team Records was born in 2005. Two years later, they were off to the races, with their marquee band attending the prestigious South By Southwest (SXSW) Festival in Austin, Texas, and generating some good press, including a *New York Times* article by Jon Pareles, 'Singing and Doing the Hustle in Austin,' (19 March 2007). Pareles wrote that bands featured at the festival included 'Lonely China Day, a band from Beijing that brought a profoundly meditative tone to songs with lyrics from ancient Chinese poetry, inexorable guitar buildups that could appeal to fans of Sigur Ros, and twitches of electronic rhythm from a laptop.' Even so, a festival showing in the USA and a few promising news clippings in the international press were not enough to propel the marquee band of Tag Team Records deeper into China.

I asked Matt what he had learned about the distribution of his records in China, and whether his label was succeeding in the China market. 'We've distributed, in total in China around 20,000 units,' he said as he took a swig of beer and scratched his big red beard:

> We're turning a profit on it. It's difficult to say exactly how many records we sell, because distribution companies in China suck, and they don't really provide you with the kind of Soundscan-oriented reports you would get back home. Certainly over 10,000 records, and there's probably still quite a lot out there on shelves or sitting in warehouses and wholesale retail venues. That is a constant battle that we go through as a label that eats up way too much of our time. Sort of fighting with distribution companies to get paid, and, beyond

that, knowing where our product is actually selling. I mean obviously if we knew something was selling well in Guangdong we'd tour heavily in Guangdong, and then try and build more of an audience. But it's tough to get real sales reports. It's a bit of a bummer, once you start dealing with these larger state-run distribution companies. Not a piece of cake.

Matt's answer pointed to the logistical challenges of operating in a landscape dominated by state-run companies, whose interests were more invested in the 'safer' world of pop music. Clearly this was also an environment in which the institutions and agencies supporting independent music had not had the time to mature and develop as they did in other markets, notably the USA and the UK. I asked Matt why it was so difficult for his label to gain traction in the China market, and what other factors were playing into the challenges of indie music distribution, and he said that the rise of internet and the ease of downloading music for free was putting a big dent in the label's sales, as it was for just about every musical artist worldwide. 'Why would the average Chinese consumer want to buy physical product when they can download it for free? In America, I guess you deal with the same thing, but it helps with promotion in some respects, there. But here in China, if somebody has something, they have it, and they're probably not going to buy it unless they're a huge.'

Matt also had some cynical insights to share about the touring circuit in China. He said that the limits of what can be achieved by bands on tour further hinder the ability of independent rock music to flourish. 'There is a tremendous lack of true touring that works here [in China],' he said. 'You're basically touring the same spots. You're obviously not going to drive on tour, you're taking trains. Equipment sucks, it bums bands out. You might show up in Nanjing and play a show in March and there'll be a full house of 600 people and you'll show up again, seven months later, and you'll get like 35 people.'

This was of course not a situation limited to China — touring is always a precarious venture when it comes to independent music. But the relatively immaturity of Chinese rock scenes outside of Beijing was a clear obstacle to the ability of indie rock music to gain traction elsewhere in the country.

As the story of Matt Kagler and Tag Team Records suggests, the indie rock movement in China was swimming upstream against a convergent flood tide of counter-forces, including a lack of sophisticated distribution methods and channels for independent music, government restrictions on music and other forms of popular culture, the rise of the internet and social media in China, and the ever-powerful flow of 'mainstream' pop music into China from Hong Kong, Taiwan and elsewhere.

Indie Rock vs. Dumbass Pop: A Conversation with Liu Miao and Gao Feng

Talking to Liu Miao and Gao Feng, the two owners of the club 2 Kolegas, also gave me some additional perspectives on the challenges that independent rock musicians face in the Chinese marketplace. For Liu Miao, the key challenge was the commercial tastes of mainstream Chinese society. He talked in his own humorous way, laced with the vulgarities that one might expect from a rocker, about how mainstream pop tunes coming into China from Hong Kong and Taiwan since the 1980s had been largely to blame for limiting the tastes of the average Chinese consumer of music. (In the process of relating his view on pop music in China, he frequently used the vulgar Chinese term *shabi* 傻逼 which translates roughly as "idiot."

Our sort of music really has its limitations with the audience. Because the music that's popular in China, especially the music from Hong Kong and Taiwan, is just shit dumb! But 100 percent of the people in China are all listening to that crappy music! So the progress of rock music is really difficult. These dumbass people listening to that dumbass music, maybe they think our music is stupid! So the development of this music is totally dependent on these people and their listening tastes. Maybe one day, somebody sees a CD of indie music on the rack and buys it thinking, 'What is this?' She buys it and goes home to listen to it, but before that she's been listening to dumbass music, and now she's spent 10 *yuan* on a new CD and her reaction is: 'What the fuck is this?' and she chucks it in the bin.

On the other hand, his partner Gao Feng saw a brighter future for rock music because of how China was opening in all areas, including music and the arts, 'So even companies that produce pop music are now investing in rock music because they see a future in it,' he said. He also pointed out that anyone in China theoretically had the ability to download music from all parts of the world for free.

Talking with some of the prime movers and shakers of China's indie rock scene in its epicenter of Beijing, I learned a great deal about the challenges and the opportunities facing them. Lao Yang provided keen insights into the nature of music production and the challenges that non-commercial music faced. Experimental sessions at Sugar Jar and the Waterland Kuanyin series at 2 Kolegas gave people the chance to hear and interact with more experimental musicians who were expanding the boundaries of what constituted music both in China and globally.

ROCKING THE CHINESE NATION

Meanwhile, D-22 club owner Michael Pettis's new venture with P.K. 14 front man Yang Haisong, the record label Maybe Mars, revealed how the right initiative and support could open new opportunities and frontiers for indie rock's expansion and consolidation in China. Over the next several years, it became clear that Maybe Mars had succeeded in its mission to produce, support, showcase and archive the albums of dozens of new experimental bands in China.

On the other hand, Matt Kagler's struggles with his indie label showed how difficult the market was for most players, particularly in terms of distribution and arranging band tours.

Yet even hardened indie musicians like Liu Miao and Gao Feng maintained some faith that the scene they supported at their club 2 Kolegas would continue to grow and that it would find a stronger purchase in China and abroad.

To do so, indie rock had to expand out of its power base in Beijing and find audiences elsewhere in the country. By following one indie rock band, SUBS, on an unforgettable journey deep into the heart of China, where they would perform in a concert with China's rock legend Cui Jian and in their hometown of Wuhan, I would discover how deeply indie rock was indeed beginning to spread through China.

4

RIDING THE RAILS ON A CHINESE ROCK ODYSSEY: ON TOUR WITH SUBS AND CUI JIAN

ROCK MUSICIANS who wish to build a career for themselves in China must travel far beyond Beijing or their own hometowns to play in clubs and in festivals in other provinces and cities. As with rock bands anywhere in the world, the journey was not an easy one. Usually, it involved spending long stretches of time on the road, either on trains or buses. Rarely did bands have the funds to fly to their destinations, and only big stars like Cui Jian got to ride in limousines. For most, going on the road to tour often involved carrying their own heavy equipment through crowded, labyrinthine train and bus stations, stuffing them into vans and cabs, and bunking in friends' apartments or backstage in the venues where they performed. They did this in the stultifying heat of summer, and in the freezing cold northern winters.

On the other hand, the road symbolized freedom. Even if the audiences were often small, touring was a crucial component of an ambitious rock band's efforts to spread their music far and wide inside, and increasingly outside, China. In the summer and fall of 2007, my journey through China's rock scenes took me with bands on the road to concerts, clubs, and festivals far beyond Beijing. The highlight was joining the hardcore rock band SUBS on a tour with Cui Jian in Hunan Province, and then to their own

SUBS band members Wu Hao (l) and Kang Mao (r) during an interview with the author near their home in Tongzhou in July 2007 (photo by Andrew Field)

hometown of Wuhan in Hubei Province. The Cui Jian Concert on the Sands in rural Hunan Province, and the SUBS concert at VOX club in Wuhan were both signs that there were was huge potential for the music at a basic level of Chinese society.

Rock's Primal Scream: An Interview with Kang Mao and Wu Hao of SUBS

During that hot and sultry night in early July 2007 when I first saw SUBS perform at the CH+INDIE Fest at 2 Kolegas, I arranged an interview with Kang Mao the following day. The band lived in Tongzhou, a satellite town located to the east of Beijing, which was about an hour's subway and then taxi ride outside of the city, past endless rows of apartment buildings under construction, topped with cranes and covered with scaffolding. Many of the city's independent artists and musicians lived out in these parts, where housing was much cheaper than in the city. They lived in communities of like-minded people on the edges of the city, which was constantly in process of expansion outward in all directions. Other than its Beijing art and music residents, Tongzhou itself was an unremarkable place marked by the uneven modernity characteristic of most of China's smaller towns, with shopping malls standing next to derelict old buildings, remnants of earlier phases of growth.

I met Kang Mao and Wu Hao in a cafe near the apartment block where they lived. Tinny Chinese pop music played on speakers in the cafe as we sipped on sugary sweet milk teas, and Kang Mao told me the story of her band and her own entry into the indie rock scene. She spoke with a somewhat nasal and gravelly voice. She was wearing a white tank top, and large white rings dangled from her ears. A tattoo of a wide-eyed cat on her shoulder was on full display. On her arm was another white bangle, well color-coordinated. She spoke rapidly as she smoked cigarettes, delicately tapping the ashes into an ashtray on the coffee table. Her eyes were wide and full of intelligence, and that day she was wearing a set of colored lenses that made her eyes appear green. Around her neck was a gold metal band. Wu Hao sat next to her listening and smoking as she talked. He was wearing a pair of jeans and a pink t-shirt with English words on the chest that read 'What music? We're in it for the DiCK'. In his own bid to achieve color coordination, he sipped on a pink strawberry shake.

'Around 1996 or '97 or thereabouts, the most representative band that we all liked was Nirvana,' Kang Mao informed me, corroborating my own memories of rock bands in Beijing at that time. She and Wu Hao came to Beijing separately, but eventually formed their own band. Kang Mao went on to relate how in the early days she would pretend to hold a microphone and sing, and 'lots of things came out'. This sounded shamanistic, like she was channeling voices from deep inside her. She laughed at this memory of herself and continued: 'So we found a drummer [Shi Xudong, the bassist for P.K. 14] and a bassist [Zhu Lei], and formed SUBS. That was in 2002. And then in 2004, we had our first performance, and we quickly earned the recognition and attention of this circle [of Beijing indie rockers]. Then in 2006 we got the opportunity to travel and tour abroad. Now we've come to today, and it's been an extremely quick process.'

She was referring to their summer 2006 tour of Scandinavia, where they received a hero's welcome in Finland, Sweden, Denmark, and Norway. Since then, the band had received numerous positive comparisons to Western punk/post-punk bands such as the Hives, Fugazi, Sigur Ros, and the Yeah Yeah Yeahs.

Though less articulate than Kang Mao, Wu Hao had his own story to tell. He spoke in a slightly lisping and hesitant voice, in contrast to his on-stage persona as a rock guitar hero. His features were delicate, and he had a puffy baby face and soft eyes framed in his longish and somewhat curly hairdo. Like Kang Mao, he spoke in non-stop run-on sentences, as he complained about how mundane his life was before he became a rock and roller:

> I worked at a factory, and every day I would get on my bicycle and head home after work, and I'd open the door hoping that something, anything, would happen. It was utterly boring. Sure, I'd get together with my mates and we'd hit the karaoke halls and play mahjong and things like that, but it was a life of sheer boredom. The only thing I liked to do was to play my guitar. And hope and pray for a more interesting life...

That simple story of boredom, ennui, and sameness is probably one that could be understood by millions of suburban and small-town youths across the planet. I could easily tell that story myself, having grown up in a small town in the USA. Now China was facing a compressed version of that story, with villages and towns all over the country drained of their populations over the course of a single generation as the so-called "Reform & Opening" Era accelerated and people migrated to the larger cities by the millions.

The decisions of Wu Hao and Kang Mao to come to Beijing to chase their rock'n'roll dreams were replicated by thousands of other Chinese youths competing in the same arena. They were starting their own rock bands in other Chinese cities, migrating to Beijing, and vying to perform on the country's most coveted stages. What gave SUBS the edge was the sheer power and force of singer Kang Mao herself, and the tightness of the band. While other singers may have had more melodious voices, no other female performer I had seen in Beijing could match the infernal energy and authenticity of her performances, no matter how well-thought-out they may appear to be in retrospect. She was clearly a performer who put her entire person into the performance, as I had witnessed the night before at 2 Kolegas and would witness again many times over the next fifteen years. To be fair, one could say the same about her bandmates. Wu Hao may have appeared somewhat diminished off stage (who doesn't?). But on stage he rocked hard, blasting out tunes and shouting out backing vocals with the same aggression, volume, and speed as any hardcore rocker in the world.

In Tongzhou, Kang Mao spoke about her own family and contrasted her situation with that of her partner, Wu Hao. As in the case of Yang Haisong, her parents were not pleased with the direction she had taken in life. In fact, that decision had caused a deep rift in their relationship. Recently she had been trying to mend fences with her mother, who had been pressing her to use her father's connections (he was a prominent academic in Wuhan) and apply for graduate school. 'My parents simply don't appreciate how much I've sacrificed to make it as far as I have to this day, to live the life that I want to live. Instead, they think that I'm stuck in a muddy hole, and they're always thinking of ways to pull me out and into the higher levels of society,' she confessed, lifting her hand upward to demonstrate how they were 'pulling' her out of the muck of her current life.

Kang Mao went on to relate how she turned an insult from her father into one of the SUBS songs:

> Every song that SUBS performs has a story behind it, like one of our early songs 'Down', in which I sing 'one two three four.' The lyrics of this song I feel weren't really written by me, but rather by my father. Because one time I returned home for spring festival and saw my parents. My dad thought that my lifestyle was very crude. He just couldn't understand it. He thought that this was a hopeless, laughable, stupid, and even low-life way of living. He held up a chicken he was preparing for dinner' [as she said this to me, she held her hand up in the air like she was holding the neck of a plucked chicken and shook it] 'and he says to me, 'Look at this chicken, you are both four nos.' I ask him, 'Why are we four nos?' and he says back to me, 'You see, you both have no money, no job, no family, and no future.' And I thought, 'Cool.'

Musically, the SUBS song 'Down' that she was describing is a simple punk rock song with an easily memorable and catchy guitar riff. In the song, which appears on their independent album of the same name, she chants out the numbers to the timing of the riff, one complete cycle for each number, and then starts the song. It is about having no money (1), no job (2), no family (3), and no future (4). Yet it is also about being happy not to have these things, happy just to be 'going down.' Kang Mao continued to discuss her situation of going downward:

> This is our life, and this is the life situation of every rocker who was born in the 1970s. When we wrote our song 'Down,' I embedded in the lyrics this notion that although I have nothing, I'm happily going downward. This is because my parents want me to pursue an upwardly mobile lifestyle, one that includes making money, but we're going downward, in opposition to them. But I'm happy to be going downward.

Certainly, Kang Mao's song was a rebellion against the wishes of her parents, and indeed of the government and society of China, which constantly urge people to relentlessly move forward and upward in rapid economic progress. Yet like so many others in China's rock scene, including Cui Jian himself, Kang Mao did not venture into the dangerous territory of making direct anti-government political statements in her songs or in her on-stage rants. The message was implied rather than stated outright. Like so many artists living and working in China, Kang Mao toed a careful line between statements about personal freedom, which were largely uplifting and positive in their nature, and statements that expressed a direct critique of government or society in China. As she told me, 'Every time I go abroad and I deal with media interviews, what I detest and fear most is when they keep asking all sorts of questions about, "Hey, you are a Chinese [rock] band, so what's the current political climate in China?"'

I asked her why she didn't like to talk about politics with western journalists.

'These are detestable questions,' she responded, 'because I feel they can ask any Chinese person. This isn't a question particularly for SUBS. We are all about our music, and I don't really want to represent a socialist country. Yes, this is a mark on us that can't be wiped clean. We grew up in this environment, and actually we don't really want to talk about these things.'

What she really appreciated, she said, was when rock music fans from abroad came up to them after a concert and told them how great their performance was, and how much they enjoyed it, and didn't press the point that this was a *Chinese* band.

Unlike many other rock bands in the Beijing scene at that time, SUBS self-produced and distributed their albums. Kang Mao served as the band's manager, and they relied on their personal networks and on word-of-mouth (the 'grapevine and the grassroots' as 13 Club manager Liu Lixin called it) to promote themselves and their music. This separated them from the pack of other indie rock bands trying to make it. It enhanced their aura of individuality and integrity by refusing to make any compromises in their music for the sake of an album's popularity. During our interview, Kang Mao even mentioned that she refused to work with well-known Chinese indie record labels, since they often manipulated musicians and bands and their musical styles for their own ends. Instead, they self-produced their albums and sold them in venues around the country where they performed, reaching their audience directly with their own musical product.

I had learned many valuable things about the band SUBS from our conversation in their residential town of Tongzhou on the outskirts of Beijing. Thus, when Kang Mao invited me to join them for a tour of Hunan with China's rock godfather Cui Jian, I took up her offer with great enthusiasm and anticipation for a rocking adventure with this indie band in the China heartlands.

Riding the Rails to Hunan with SUBS (26 and 27 July 2007)
How could I refuse such an offer? They were traveling to Hunan to perform with Cui Jian in a festival organized by Hunan Satellite TV, one of the most successful and innovative TV stations in China. On the afternoon of July 26, I arrived at the monumental Beijing West Railway Station with its pagoda-shaped roof towers echoing the Forbidden City and its main brick structure looking like a massive city wall. It was blazing hot outside and numerous groups of migrant workers and farmers from far away were gathered with their belongings in plastic bags, squatting or sitting on their stuff as they waited for their trains to arrive. An elderly woman with gnarled features, dressed in a dark blue jacket reminiscent of earlier times, and with a white rag on her head to beat the heat, walked around with a wooden cane. She carried a burlap sack as she approached group after group, begging for small change. In my mind, this woman represented the people left behind by the rapid and overwhelming tide of social and economic changes in the country since the Reform Era began. Meanwhile, in a frenzy of activity, thousands of people heading off to or returning from all parts of the country passed by carting their belongings in tow.

Moments later, I was inside the station's grand entranceway, waiting for the band to arrive. Kang Mao, Wu Hao and Zhang Shun all appeared at the gate and passed their belongings through the security check. They saw me filming them and burst into laughter as they gathered their gear and headed deeper into the station. Kang Mao and Wu Hao were wearing the exact same outfits as on the day I interviewed them. Zhang Shun the drummer was dressed all in black, carrying a green rucksack and toting what appeared to be a set of cymbals. Wu Hao had his beat-up brown guitar case all covered with stickers, and Kang Mao wore a sky-blue backpack and held on to a bag full of snacks to be consumed during the overnight train ride to Changsha, provincial capital of Hunan.

Towing their own instruments and equipment with them, the three band members made their way downstairs to the platform to board the train. The long-haired and muscular bassist Zhu Lei was already on board. He greeted us in the cabin with his usual ear-to-ear grin. Among the four band members, he seemed to be the most easy-going. The four of them were sharing a soft sleeper cabin, the most comfortable class of cabin in the train, featuring four bunk beds, courtesy no doubt of the largess of Hunan Satellite TV. I was in a neighboring cabin, but I spent most of my time in their cabin chatting and eating and hanging out with the four band members as we made our way across the Chinese rural landscape, heading south by southwest. The band members munched on the food that they had prepared for the journey, which included cuts of dried meat, bread, fruits, and other snacks.

I had brought along a cheap acoustic guitar I had bought earlier that summer at a music store in Beijing, and I gave it Wu Hao to play. He took a bite out of an apple and handed it over to Zhu Lei on the opposite bunk, who took another bite. Wu Hao immediately picked up my guitar and started playing around, trying out a few different chord progressions and bass lines that provided an elegant soundtrack to the landscape of trees and farms that was now rushing by us in the window of our cabin. There was a mixture of country, folk, rock, and later some tunes sounding vaguely like Central Asian desert music emanating from the guitar as Wu Hao strummed and picked away at it. He then started humming a tune to go with his playing. He was not singing any actual words, just nonsensical syllables like a small child would make, but it sounded like a song and started shaping up into some recognizable chord progressions. There was a feeling of freedom and simple pleasure to his song—it was a road song for sure.

Kang Mao came into the cabin and sat down opposite Wu Hao. Presently she was singing along with him, doing some chants and making 'uh uh' sounds as he strummed away in rhythm with the train ride. They later explained that this was usually how they came up with their songs, and then Kang Mao added the lyrics. This process of 'from the gut' singing and strumming sounded very similar to how Guai Li singer Wen Jun had described her own band's songwriting process, and indeed this process would be familiar to songwriters and bands all over the world.

There were half-consumed beers on the small table between the bunks of the soft sleeper cabin. Zhu Lei was leaning back listening to tunes on his headphones. Kang Mao was rooting around the bags looking for Chinese medicine. She put on a collared shirt with cute animals, suns, and other symbols all over it in multiple colors—the outfit of a shaman. Wu Hao started playing the tune of 'I Want to Hold Your Hand' by the Beatles, and he and Kang Mao were now singing the tune without knowing the actual lyrics, but giving an accurate rendition of the melody. He then switched to a soulful performance of Lennon and McCartney's slow and haunting ballad 'And I Love Her.' Even many years later, it is hard for me to reconcile the hardcore rock personas that these rockers cultivated onstage with these pleasant and intimate scenes during one of my most unforgettable train journeys in China.

The next morning, we awoke to a changed landscape, a gentler one of rolling green hills and ponds and rivers and brick-house villages. It was a wet and verdant landscape, in contrast

ROCKING THE CHINESE NATION

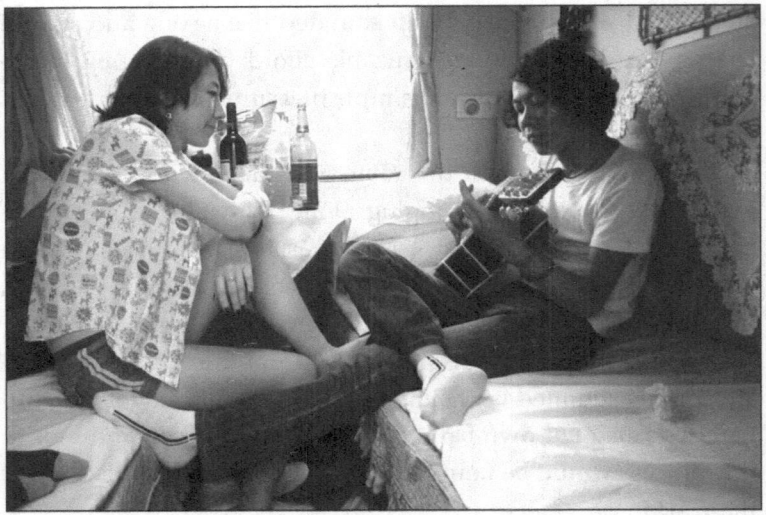

Kang Mao and Wu Hao sharing a creative moment on the train from Beijing to Changsha in July 2007 (photo by Andrew Field)

to the drier and dustier landscape of northern China. We were now getting close to our destination of Changsha, in the province that gave birth to Chairman Mao and one of the world's most thoroughgoing revolutions. Wu Hao and Kang Mao rose out of their cabin and washed their faces in the train cabin's sink. Female train attendants came by to empty out the trash bin and deliver breakfast foods to the passengers. In the early morning sunlight, Kang Mao's face was lit up in orange as she nibbled on her breakfast, chatting with Wu Hao who was doing the same. Tenderly, she fed Wu Hao from her seat across him in the cabin as the orange sunlight streamed in through the window.

Gradually, the scene passing by the window became more urbanized, and tall buildings started to appear. We were now heading into the city of Changsha. It was as developed and modernized as any other in China, with row after row of apartment buildings, office towers and shopping centers passing by the train windows. Upon arrival at the station, we disembarked and headed out of the crowded station into the blistering heat. We were soon whisked away by two young representatives of Hunan Satellite TV, the sponsor of the concert featuring Cui Jian and SUBS and another band called The Verse, to a four-star hotel. There, we were treated to a lavish lunch of spicy Hunanese cuisine in the hotel restaurant.

The members of the Hunan Satellite TV team chatted amiably with the SUBS band members, who peppered them with questions about the quality of the equipment and the recording of the concert. The crew assured the band that they were taking very seriously the quality of the sound equipment at the concert venue, though the band members were skeptical. Yet because the venue was too far away, they would be unable to check their equipment prior to the actual concert. As the crew explained, the concert was to take place in a sandy area in the middle of Hunan about a four-hour drive north of Changsha. There would be hundreds of tents for the audience of thousands, most of whom would spend the night at the site of the concert.

A Radio Interview with Rock Godfather Cui Jian (27 July 2007)
That afternoon we were taken by van to the Hunan Satellite TV station, where we bumped into Cui Jian in the elevator as we make our way up to the top floor station. He was wearing black pants, a black t-shirt, and a red baseball cap with a black pair of Ray Ban shades perched on his cap. A little mustache hovered over his upper lip. He asked me in fluent English if I was German. I shook my head and told him I was American. With my blond hair, I am often mistaken for a German in China. We got off the elevator together and headed into the station, where they were going to record a conversation with the musicians for broadcasting on the Hunan Satellite TV radio station. The recording studio itself was cased in glass windows with a 270-degree view of the city below.

ROCKING THE CHINESE NATION

A gaggle of reporters with cameras were waiting for Cui Jian as he made his grand entrance amidst the clicking of cameras and the whirring of shutters. Cui Jian took a seat next to the interviewer, a young woman from Changsha, who welcomed him on behalf of her city. Kang Mao sat down opposite her, and Huang Bo, the male singer and bandleader of The Verse, also took a seat and donned headphones. The interviewer began by introducing Cui Jian to the radio audience, and then moved on to introduce Huang Bo, who it turned out was from Changsha as well. She then introduced Kang Mao to her audience. The interview lasted around an hour.

During the interview, the female host asked Cui Jian to tell the audience why he believed music was important. He replied in his low, gruff, and guttural voice:

> It seems that making music and being a pop star, and making a lot of money, is what the lifestyle of mainstream music is all about. But this ignores the real purpose of music. From music, one can experience the joy of living. You will naturally know where your soul is, just like taking a breath of air. Suddenly you take a deep breath, like you've never taken a deep breath before, and you get the goose bumps. I think music is like your soul taking a deep breath. If you do deep breathing often, your soul will come alive, and you will discover its existence.

Cui Jian's response reflected his philosophy of music as a 'soul searching' journey rather than an effort to earn fame or money (although it seemed he had plenty of both). Like George Harrison and many other musicians who expressed similar philosophies, Cui Jian did not completely eschew the material

SUBS band member (left to right) Zhang Shun, Wu Hao, Kang Mao, and Zhu Lei posing outside the hotel in Changsha before getting on the bus to the concert site in July 2007. Behind them is a banner welcoming Cui Jian, SUBS, and The Verse to the hotel (photo by Andrew Field)

rewards, privileges, and fame that his music had brought him. Nevertheless, his message was borne out in the music that he later performed to the crowd on the sands.

The interviewer then turned to Kang Mao and asked her, as the representative of a new generation of indie rock musicians, what she had to say about rock music.

'I think that what rock music has taught me is how to think for myself, and to choose the life I want to live,' was her simple response. Naturally these musicians had a lot more to say to their audience, but these are the bits that seemed to capture the essence of what each artist felt about their musical journey.

A Bus Ride with SUBS Deep into the Heartland of Hunan for the Concert on the Sands with Cui Jian (28 July 2007)

The next morning, we were off to the site of the venue on a four-hour ride deep into the Hunan hinterland. Cui Jian rode separately in a black car with black windows, but all the other band members in the concert were on the bus as we made our way north along the main highway. Mostly, the band members took the opportunity to rest up for the long evening ahead.

Halfway there, we stopped along the highway at a gas station, and everyone trooped off the bus to take a bathroom break. SUBS bassist Zhu Lei was washing his face in an outdoor sink, and I came over and asked him what he thought of Hunan.

'Hunan? My current impression is that it's hot. It's the heat of July. The bus is crowded and my back aches from sitting in it,' he said, smiling and grinning as he splashed water on his face.

I went over to Kang Mao and asked her if she had anything to say. 'Mother fuck!' was her immediate response in English, presumably to the pounding heat of the midday sun and the unexpectedly long, tiresome bus ride. She stood in the shade of the bus taking a drag on her cigarette. She was wearing a black skirt, a red t-shirt with the face of a cat on it, and her multicolored collared button-down shaman's shirt with various symbols on it. She had on a pair of white-framed sunglasses to match her bangles. We got back on the bus and continued driving along the highway toward our destination. At one point, I let Kang Mao borrow my iPod and listen to Tom Petty's latest album *Highway Companion*, which seemed especially appropriate to that moment. She smiled as she listened and rocked along to the music in her seat on the bus next to Wu Hao as we cruised northward to the sands.

About three hours into our journey, the bus turned off onto a small road heading into the countryside. It was an elevated dirt road surrounded by farms and irrigated rice fields, and we moved purposefully towards green hills in the distance, following a long cavalcade of cars all bound for the same location. We passed by bogs with water buffalos resting in the water to beat the summer heat. The road became narrow and bumpy, and it was a miracle that the driver of the huge bus could navigate such a narrow track, but he managed to get us up into the hills and to our destination: a large manmade expanse of white sand flats surrounded by verdant hills in the heart of the Hunan countryside.

The late afternoon sun was blazing as we walked across the sands to the site where the concert would be held. The wind blew tiny micro-grains of white sand into our eyes, noses, mouths and hair. Ahead, we could see the concert stage set up in the middle of the sands, where hundreds of people were already gathered from surrounding villages to watch what was probably the first and only rock concert they had ever witnessed. Cui Jian's car drove right up to the back of the stage, and he remained inside the air-conditioned car the entire afternoon. This was as close to rock star treatment as it got in China. The rest of the bands headed into a large tent backstage to await the sound checks. The concert stage was backed by an impressive scaffolding topped with lights and speakers. It was a grand stage, fit for the king of Chinese rock.

Dozens of cars were already parked on the sands, and by late afternoon hundreds of people were occupying the area, taking in various forms of recreation as they awaited the concert. Despite the pounding heat, a group of men kicked a football around on the sand, where goals were set up for a game. Bright yellow tents by the hundreds were lined up in rows. Guards by the dozen dressed in blue uniforms and wearing caps ringed the concert grounds. Local villagers collected discarded water bottles, while vendors sold new ones under green and blue umbrellas decorated with the logo of Red Bull — one of the main sponsors of this concert festival. People found shade where they could, resting under canopies and umbrellas. People of all ages were there, from elderly folk to young children running around the grounds. Many of them had walked from nearby villages, while others had driven hundreds of kilometers to attend this concert. This certainly qualified as the 'other China' that Yang Haisong spoke to me about.

I paused under the shade of an umbrella to talk to some people about the concert.

'Have you seen Cui Jian perform before?' I asked a young lady dressed in jean shorts and a white t-shirt, with a beige baseball cap and sunglasses.

'You mean live?' she asked. I nodded. 'I haven't seen him perform live before,' she replied.

'And what sort of expectation do you have for this concert?' I pursued.

'I hope we'll have a good time, and that we'll experience firsthand the craziness of what happens on stage,' she smiled.

'So have you seen SUBS?' I asked her.

'Who?'

'There are three bands performing tonight,' I explained.

'Well, actually I don't really know much about rock and roll', she admitted and shrugged.

A voice from below interjected, 'That's because you're old.' Everyone laughed. It was apparently her husband, a man with short spiky hair squatting on the ground drinking a bottle of water. She laughed and slapped him on the head with a newspaper she was holding.

I asked him if he knew anything about rock music. 'I'm even older than her,' he joked, and she laughed along with him.

'So what do you think about rock music?' I asked him. He stood up and shook his head. 'I need to hear it first and then I'll have thoughts,' he confessed sheepishly. 'I need to feel the atmosphere of the live concert to understand it,' he continued, 'and once the music starts, my thoughts will be many.'

I asked him where he was from and he replied that he came from the Jiangxi Province, but was working in Changsha. I continued to ask them about SUBS, but naturally they had not heard of it. I told them that I would come back and talk to them again after they had seen SUBS perform, but which I knew it would be a hopeless task given the size of the crowd.

I then wandered around the grounds and found a small pond on the edge of the sands, where people were bathing or wetting their clothing, until the guards hired for the concert came and told them to get out of the water. Everyone was trying to find a way to escape the heat of this artificial desert as we waited for the bands to go through their sound checks.

The sun went down, leaving the sky all orange and lavender blue, and Cui Jian and his band mounted the stage for their sound check. Cui Jian was wearing a dark pair of shorts and a yellow-orange t-shirt along with his red baseball cap. With the big orange sun setting behind him, he looked like an over-aged schoolboy with his guitar strapped on. He was joined by his veteran band members who included Liu Yuan, a Beijinger known as much for his contributions to the Beijing jazz scene as to rock. Wearing glasses and dressed in khaki pants and a brown work shirt, with an Irish cap on, and playing various wind instruments, he looked like a beatnik from the 1950s. Eddie Randriamampionona, the lead guitarist of the band, hailed from Madagascar and was one of a number of kids of Madagascan embassy staff who started a musical career in Beijing. He had been a member of Cui Jian's band since the earliest days in the mid-1980s. He was wearing a pair of faded jeans, a red shirt, and a black baseball cap. The ensemble also included a drummer, bassist, and a percussionist.

By this point, hundreds of people had gathered around the edge of the stage to watch the bands warm up and test out their equipment. SUBS come up on stage next and did their own sound check. By now, the security guards had cordoned off an area of around twenty meters in front of the stage, forcing the audience to hang back. The hills were now silhouetted against the darkening sky and the tension was mounting as the audience, much larger now and in the thousands, became impatient for the show to begin. Dozens of security guards were lined up in a row between the audience and the stage.

It turned out that Cui Jian and Hunan Satellite TV had a relationship going back several years. From what I gathered later, Hunan Satellite, one of the most progressive and successful TV stations in China — all state-owned — was the first station to air a Cui Jian concert since he was virtually banned from television not long after the protest movement of 1989. During the 1990s, Cui Jian certainly could not perform rock music in big concert venues in Beijing, and he was relegated to playing jazz in the CD Cafe off the Third Ring Road in eastern Beijing (which I visited many times when I was living there in 1996). He was also unofficially banned from the airwaves. Hunan Satellite was the first station to test this ban, broadcasting a studio performance of Cui Jian and his band in 2000. Now, we were about to witness a concert performed in front of thousands of Hunanese and many others who made the trek to this venue, and which would be televised to an audience of tens of millions around China. Since Cui Jian was still a politically controversial figure, I was told, he was asked not to perform certain songs, and the cordon of security guards was more than just a safety deterrent. Yet this concert was nonetheless an indication that the relationship between China's government and more 'radical' art forms such as rock music had changed over the past decade. Clearly there was support from the Hunan authorities for this concert, even though it was taking place in such a remote location deep in rural Hunan.

As the sun sets and the sky begins to darken, the band SUBS warms up on stage at the July 2007 Concert on the Sands festival site, in front of an already large crowd (photo by Andrew Field)

Opening Acts: The Verse and SUBS

Finally, after all that preparation, the sky had turned dark, and the concert was ready to begin. The first band to mount the stage was The Verse, led by the Hunanese singer Huang Bo. The Verse was a Beijing-based funk band that featured a sizeable number of musicians and singers. An announcer came on stage to introduce the concert and the band. He was a young man in army fatigues and a blue t-shirt. He welcomed everyone to the concert and announced, 'Tonight we are meeting together under the lovely moon on the largest expanse of man-made sands in southern China, to witness an extremely romantic and extremely lively rock concert.' He then invited the mayor of the township of Linxiang to join him on stage in opening the concert. The mayor gave a speech thanking everyone for coming and thanked all the various organizations that coordinated to put this event together as a showcase for the region's travel and leisure industry. This was an example of how local Party leaders were involved in commercial enterprises, and a reflection of the commercial potential of rock concerts to attract people to areas promoting tourism. The crowd cheered the mayor and the entire audience was lit up in red by spotlights shining upon them from the stage.

Three young male announcers came on stage to rev up the crowd and start the show. They were showered in dusty sand as they gave their speeches. Sand was blowing and flying everywhere in the red light, making the whole scene look eerily apocalyptic. Finally, the members of The Verse came on stage and began their performance. They launched into a series of covers of Parliament, James Brown, and other American funk bands from the 1960s and '70s. The band featured a four-part horn section and two female singers backing up the lead vocalist. It was a fun show, and it put the audience in a festive mood.

As the members of The Verse finished their act and gave their final bows, the four members of SUBS were readying themselves. I approached Kang Mao behind the stage and asked her if she had ever performed before such a large audience. She looked nervous and alert.

'Yes, the audiences in Europe were as big, but they were foreigners. Chinese audiences are hard to figure out,' she replied. 'They've come here to see stars, and they really don't understand rock and roll.'

The band members did their final pre-show warm up on the side of the stage. Zhu Lei was windmilling his arms around and the others were jumping up and down to get their adrenaline going. Then on cue, they mounted the stage and took up their positions.

In front of the stage, fountains of sparks went off and the show was on. Kang Mao started by giving a short speech to the audience: "Friends from Changsha, maybe this is the first time you've ever seen a punk rock concert. The only difference for me is that I first heard this music a little earlier than you. Whether it's rock and roll or punk music, what it's telling us is that anybody can now take up an instrument and sing their own songs, songs of freedom. Tonight at this concert, nobody else can take your place and feel the burning heat of the music. Are you ready?"

The audience shouted back in the affirmative. 'Please yell into the microphone,' she shouted, holding her mic out to the audience. A cheer erupted. 'Again!' The cheer grew louder. 'Yet again, even louder!' The audience complied. Wu Hao turned up his amplifier, Kang Mao shouted, 'This is SUBS!' and the band launched into their first song.

Soon, Kang Mao was screaming and thrashing about on center stage, backed by the shouts of Wu Hao and Zhu Lei who surround her on either side. During their concert, they played most of the songs from their latest self-produced album, *Down*, along with some more recent ones that would go on their next album. Zhang Shun held steady on the drums at the back of the large stage. It was hard to tell at first how the audience was reacting to SUBS and their style of music. Looking at the crowd, one could see a range of expressions from mild amusement to incredulity. As usual, Kang Mao's performance included bouts of screaming, shouting, going down on her knees, falling as if in a faint, and wrapping the microphone cord around her neck as if to hang herself. In the red light and high heat with sand blowing about everywhere, and with Kang Mao screaming at the top of her lungs, the whole scene felt infernal.

They finished a song and the crowd cheered, but Kang Mao did not seem to feel this was a genuine response, and she chided them. She and Zhu Lei exhorted the audience to dance to the music. Some of them obliged, jumping up and down, but this was a crowd of thousands of people pressed tightly against each other and it was difficult for them to move around. The crowd was mixed, mostly young adults but quite a few old timers and many children as well. It would be hard to imagine what would happen if the kind of dancing that went on in their usual rock club concerts happened here on the sands, with an audience of this sheer size and diversity. Yet here in rural Hunan, despite the intensity of the heat, or perhaps because of it, and despite the extreme nature of SUBS's music, the crowd was relatively subdued. People danced and clapped in place as the band played on. Mostly this was spectacle. Hundreds of people had their cameras out and were clicking away as Kang Mao, Zhu Lei, and Wu Hao whirled about on stage.

At the end of their concert, Kang Mao and her bandmates were spent, sweat dripping down from their hair, their energy exhausted. They seemed to have won over the audience with the sheer force of their music and of Kang Mao's on-stage persona, even if the music was not what they had been expecting. At the end of their concert, somebody delivered a bouquet of white roses to Kang Mao on stage, and she made a spectacle of walking over to the audience and flinging the roses one by one to them amidst their cheers. The three male announcers came back on stage and invited her over to say a few last words. She was happy to oblige.

'I hope that this first experience of punk rock has not been a nightmare for you all, but rather an awakening. This is the "tiger salad" that comes before the main course, preparing your appetite for the big meal. I hope you'll remember this for a long time!'

She was referring to an appetizer popular in these parts of China consisting of a raw salad mixed with hot peppers. The main course was Cui Jian.

Cui Jian

After the SUBS concert ended, the crowd was anxious to see the godfather of Chinese rock. The announcers exhorted the crowd

Cui Jian and his band performing at the Concert on the Sands in Hunan in July 2007. In the foreground is Cui Jian's longtime guitarist Eddie. Behind Cui Jian on saxophone is Liu Yuan (photo by Andrew Field)

to chant and scream out his name in anticipation of his arrival on stage. Finally, amidst a huge wave of cheers, Cui Jian and his band climbed the stage and picked up their instruments. Eddie, the guitarist, started the show with a long bluesy series of riffs that echoed across the sands, while the others got ready and in position. Cui Jian had changed into a white t-shirt and a white baseball cap with a red five-pointed star. Eddie was wearing a bandana on his head to capture the sweat. He and Cui Jian started playing together and the drummer joined in. It was a heavy bluesy riff that sounded like it could have come straight out of Chicago. Liu Yuan started blowing his baritone sax as Cui Jian began his first song. It was a song called 'Let Me Run Wild in the Snow' (让我在雪上撒点野), a classic tune from the band's early days. The rest of the concert was a mix of oldies and newer tunes from Cui Jian's latest album. Many people in the vast crowd sang along to the golden oldies, which included 'Girl from the Boudoir' (花房姑娘) from his earliest album *Nothing to*

Local villagers young and old and others from Hunan and nearby provinces who have made the journey to the site by car enjoy the performance of Cui Jian and his band during the Concert on the Sands in July 2007 (photo by Andrew Field)

My Name 一无所有, and danced to his more recent songs, which had a rap influence to them. Even though Cui Jian was a legend in China, still it was surprising to see how many people in the crowd seemed to know the lyrics to his older songs. Women in the crowd swooned as they did in the 1980s, when he first took to the public stage. Amidst the swirling sands, the concert lasted another hour or so, and then the cars and buses revved up on the sands for a great procession outward, and a long midnight ride back to Changsha began.

A Journey with SUBS to their Hometown of Wuhan in Hubei Province
The following morning, I met up with the members of SUBS to embark on the next stage of our musical journey. This time we were heading by train in second-class seats to their hometown of Wuhan, where they were going to perform to a local crowd of friends and rock enthusiasts. During the three-hour journey, I

chatted with drummer Zhang Shun about the concert the night before. He shared with me his cynical view about 'Old Cui', whom he felt had lost his mojo over the years and had gone too commercial—a once ferocious tiger declawed and defanged, who now played in a cage. This was a common sentiment that I heard from many of the younger musicians in the China indie scene. Kang Mao and Wu Hao were too busy watching episodes of the American TV cartoon *Futurama* on their video deck to participate in this conversation, while Zhu Lei catnapped in his own seat.

We arrived in Wuhan, a large industrial city also located in China's heartland, in Hubei Province along the Yangzi River. As we disembarked from the train upon our arrival at Wuhan Station, the sweltering summer heat was almost unbearable. It was a reminder that Wuhan is considered one of the 'four furnaces' of China. We quickly found a cab and climbed in and rode to the university district of the city, where SUBS were scheduled to perform later in the evening at a local club called VOX. After passing through the city with the usual brigade of construction cranes and rising buildings, we took a narrow road lined with trees that formed a causeway across a body of water. Kang Mao was chatting with the female driver in the local dialect, her face beaming with pleasure.

We soon found ourselves in the university district. We stopped at the address of club VOX, the premier rock club in Wuhan. A young man with spiky hair wearing only a pair of long black shorts with his upper body bare greeted the band members outside. Obviously, he was an old friend, and he grabbed some of their gear and ushered them into the club. As they all caught up, I took the opportunity to check out club VOX. Ensconced in a busy residential neighborhood with high rises and commercial services, the club was inside a nondescript building, whose ground floor featured a range of shops, a hair salon, a teahouse and restaurant, a bank, and an internet café. Above the entrance to the club was a neon sign shaped like a vinyl disk with the letters V O X in red letters reading vertically down in the middle of the disk. It was backed by a black square. Below this sign was another sign in Chinese and English saying 声音bar or 'sound'.

Walking up a flight of stairs, one entered the club on the second floor of the building. The main hall featured a black-and-white checkered floor about five by ten meters. A smallish stage at the end was elevated around one meter high, like the stage at 2 Kolegas in Beijing. Behind the stage, the wall was painted with red and black vertical stripes. A modest sound system consisting of vertically stacked speakers on the edge of the stage and some speakers hanging above the stage completed the scene. Simple wooden chairs and tables were arrayed around the edges of the main hall, and above was a balcony area with more seating. At the other end of the hall was a pool table and behind that were a few booths facing the windows looking out onto the street.

I headed upstairs to check out the balcony areas. The walls were all black chalkboards covered in colorful graffiti that guests had scribbled using different colors of chalk. The graffiti mainly consisted of phrases and names in various languages, including of course Chinese and English as well as French, Spanish, German, and a few other European languages as well as Arabic and some other non-alphabetic scripts. I looked around and read some of the things people had written on the walls:

> 'I love VOX' in pink
> 'Shit happens! Again!' in blue
> 'nice fuck' in yellow
> 'Teemu from Finland' in large blue letters
> 'Better to have loved and lost than never to have loved at all' in white

'Tom hope you can stay in Wuhan!' in purple
'I'm Uyghur' in green
'Shirley I miss u so much' in blue
'Das dritie reich ihr betraite der fuhrer sein!' in red
'C'est la vie' in red
'Tseung Wa has being here' in pink
'Only hookers light their own cigarettes' in red.

Taken together they composed a colorful set of beatnik poems, clichés, slogans, and mementos penned by alcohol, cigarette, and hormone-fueled youths of many nations who frequented this club. Many of them were presumably students from Wuhan University and the other universities nearby.

The performance schedule appeared on another board in black letters with a yellow background, with Chinese on the left side and English on the right. Above the schedule, an English sign read 'Voice of Youth Voice of Freedom' in red script letters. All the concerts start at 8:30 pm and cost a 25 RMB entrance fee to attend. The schedule read:

July 1: Die in Velvet (Hong Kong hardcore band) with AVOKUBO
July 3: Spiral Cow (Dalian rock) with Hualun
July 6: P.K. 14 (Beijing punk) with AVOKUBO
July 20: Squwak and Defiant Scum (Hong Kong punk)
July 26: Blins Stereo (Denmark rock)
July 29: SUBS (Beijing punk hardcore)

Clearly club VOX was part of a transnational circuit of rock clubs that connected Wuhan to the rock scenes in Beijing and Hong Kong as well as featuring occasional visits from foreign bands.

The SUBS band members dropped their belongings and

equipment off at the club, and then headed back outside into the heat of the afternoon to forage for food. They had been waiting for this moment to enjoy the local culinary delights that they grew up with, all those years ago before they left to seek their rock and roll dreams in Beijing. We passed through a dense tenement district of open street markets with vendors under umbrellas and makeshift awnings selling watermelons and other seasonal fruits, before heading into a hole-in-the-wall restaurant that served Wuhan's famous street dish: dry hot noodles (热干面). The female proprietor scooped the steaming noodles out of the cooking pot and put them into five paper bowls, then ladled a brown sauce on top of them. We sat down at the table and dug in. The noodles tasted delicious in the summer heat, especially when washed down with a cold green Fanta soda. There would be plenty more feasting to come as we settled briefly into the Wuhan way of life.

Later that evening we returned to touch base at the club. By night, the neon signs on the street were all ablaze, and the VOX club sign was lit up in red letters. The club manager asked Kang Mao to sign a wooden slat with the SUBS band name on it, which was screwed to the wall along with dozens of other wooden slats featuring the names of other bands that had performed at VOX. She obliged and scrawled her name next to the SUBS sign. This ritual reminded me somehow of the practice of inscribing name plates at a Japanese temple.

We then made our way to a neighboring restaurant, all lit up with the usual fluorescent lighting, to have dinner with some friends of the SUBS band members. When we returned to the club to begin the concert, the place was already filling up with a mix of Chinese and foreign youths, most of whom indeed looked like students. Some of them hung out at the bar where beers could be had for 15 or 20 *yuan*. Others played pool while waiting for the show to begin. The tables and booths were beginning to fill up with beer-swilling rock enthusiasts, mostly young men but also a fair share of women. More familiar faces piled into the club and Kang Mao, Wu Hao, Zhu Lei and Zhang Shun hung out near the pool table catching up with their old mates. Clearly, they were in their element here at VOX club, enjoying their triumphal return as one of the bigger success stories of the Wuhan rock music scene.

SUBS Concert at VOX (29 July 2007)

At last, the time came for the band to mount the stage and begin their concert. The audience had swelled to around one hundred people, and most of them were standing near the stage as Kang Mao took the mic and introduced the band in her raspy voice. 'Okay everyone, relax, it's time for our performance. We are SUBS!' she screamed and the whole club erupted into cheers. Clearly this crowd had been waiting for their hometown heroes to return to their rightful stage. And for the band, this intimate scene full of friends and familiar faces and young people who really knew and appreciated rock music was a welcome contrast to the Cui Jian Concert on the Sands extravaganza the night before.

Almost immediately, young student types, both male and female, were dancing in the whirling vortex that formed right in front of Kang Mao. They were smiling and appeared to be very excited and happy as they collided into each other. Some of the young women just stood there looking at Kang Mao as if they were star-struck, while others danced about with the boys. The band performed their song 'Down.' As described earlier, Kang Mao opens the song by calling out 'one…two…three…four'. Perhaps the meaning of the song was lost on most of the crowd, yet certainly they grasped the rebellious spirit and energy of the song as they moved around the floor, converting the energy of SUBS music into the kinetics of dance.

SUBS finished their concert at VOX with Kang Mao ranting and raging on stage, her fist raised and head shaking as she made her points through her songs. Hanging on her neck was a five-pointed star, a not-so-veiled symbolic reference to the Party she did not want to talk about in her interviews with foreign media. It was the same star that Cui Jian had been wearing on his cap the night before, the same star that appears on the flag of the country in which they were born and raised and in which they rocked and rolled the night away. The audience was communing deeply with the band at this stage, and the diehard fans were all pressed up against the stage.

At a cue from Kang Mao, the band erupted into their new song 'Ha!' which got the crowd dancing in a frenzy. This was a particularly violent, screamy song on Kang Mao's part and it was amazing that her vocal cords survived intact every time she sang it. It was a true rage against the machine, though precisely what she was raging against wasn't clear unless you read the lyrics. The song appears on their album *We Haven't Entered the 21st Century* which was released the following year (2008). What emerges out of the lyrics is a voice that is deeply cynical about not only the country's rapid development but that of the entire world. The 'development' of the country is just pushing our collective garbage into bigger and deeper holes and creating monumental amounts of waste, which is going into the air and water and angering the god of nature. The garbage could be metaphorical of course, but it could very well be real.

Not long after that, Beijing went through a series of 'red alerts' for its off-the-charts smog, global warming is now truly on the minds of the world's governments and industries, and like Kang Mao herself, we are all beginning to realize that we seem to have dug ourselves deep into a hole that perhaps we cannot escape from no matter what is done. The SUBS song 'Ha!' thus joins the annals of some of the great protest songs of the age, a true helpless rage against a world of rampant and endless consumption and waste production of our industrial, oil-dependent civilization that we didn't create and that we can't stop.

After-Party and Reflections on the Spiritual Dimensions of Rock Music Culture

After the SUBS concert in Club VOX was over, Kang Mao, Wu Hao, Zhang Shun, and Zhu Lei and their friends headed out to enjoy a post-concert feast at a nearby street market featuring outdoor barbeque cookouts, known in Chinese as *shaokao* 烧烤. In the heat of the late summer night, the band members joined around twenty people around a large outdoor table. There, they were feted with a seemingly endless parade of dishes, including stacks of metal skewers of barbequed vegetables and meats and other tasty morsels such as beans soaked in sauce, sautéed vegetables, fish and rice piled high on plates. The group looked bohemian, with some of the guys sporting long hair. Amidst the copious flow of beers and whiskey (a bottle of Jack Daniels was quickly emptied) and endless cigarettes, the SUBS band members and their companions chatted joyously, arms around each other's shoulders. Zhang Shun was looking particularly relaxed now; he had no shirt on, and like the other SUBS band members he was still dripping in sweat.

'Where are we?' I asked him.

'In heaven!' was his reply.

I asked the same question of Kang Mao and she replied, 'We're in paradise! But tonight, paradise is rather hot!'

The Concert on the Sands that I attended on my journey with

ROCKING THE CHINESE NATION

SUBS provided a special window into the religious dimensions of rock music, as performed live on a grand stage. With its ability to channel raw emotions of joy, sadness, anger, loss, and so forth and compress them into 3 to 5-minute bouts of shock therapy, rock music is a deeply primal form of communication and one that seems to have a universal appeal. Even if those people who witnessed the concert in Hunan were not rushing out to the nearest record shop to buy Cui Jian and SUBS albums (which they wouldn't find in any case), their reactions during the concert revealed how deeply they related to the music with their bodies and minds, and how closely engaged they were emotionally with the performances, even if many of them had never seen a rock concert let alone a hardcore punk band before.

Kang Mao's ability to win over the audience, despite the hard-to-digest 'tiger's salad' of their music, was indicative of the power of this art form to reach out to a wide and diverse audience and take them on a cathartic journey. She played the role of a shaman well, leading her audience on a journey into the depths of their souls, joining the universal mythos of rock culture and the cults that grew up around rock music worldwide. In *The Doors*, directed by Oliver Stone, before their famous peyote trip into the desert, Val Kilmer's version of Jim Morrison taunts the crowd from atop a car outside the Whisky-A-Gogo club in LA, screaming 'How many of you people know you're alive?' Kang Mao seemed to be giving her audience a similar message in her onstage performances. As did Cui Jian and his band.

Kang Mao and Cui Jian, with their potent messages of personal freedom and the power of music to free the soul, were carrying on a brave tradition of rock gospel as they made their way deep into China's heartland. The visceral performances of Kang Mao and SUBS were amplified inside the small rock club of VOX, where they exposed Chinese youths to the raw power of their rock music. Some of these youths may have followed Kang Mao's exhortation to take up their own instruments, sing their own songs and form their own bands. Over the next two decades, Wuhan continued to produce some of the most exciting punk and post-punk rock bands in China's indie scene, including AV Okubo, which also played VOX that summer.

Fifteen years later, Wuhan and its signature club VOX were still considered a prime incubator of punk and post-punk bands before they stepped out into the wider world. Outdoor music festivals such as the Concert on the Sands were also an important way for indie rock bands to reach out to bigger audiences in China, and over the next few months and years, I witnessed many more of them. Yet these festivals could not exist in China without the presence of local rock clubs in Chinese cities to nurture and incubate new bands. A symbiotic relationship thereby existed between the small world of 'underground' rock clubs and the larger stage of outdoor concerts and festivals.

Chinese Rock on a Global Stage: The Beijing Pop Festival (10 and 11 September 2007)

Later that year, I had a chance to spend some more time with SUBS and see another performance by Cui Jian and his band, which took place at a music festival in Beijing. This time, Kang Mao and Wu Hao were in the audience, not on stage, as we watched a wide array of performers both local and international. In 2007, Beijing not only boasted the most active rock scene in China, it was also the leading platform for music festivals. The Beijing Pop Festival held in September 2007 offered me another opportunity to gauge the popularity of rock music in China. It gave local Chinese bands the chance to perform on the same stage with well-known bands from abroad. The lead organizer of the Beijing Pop Festival was an American rock promoter named Jason Magnus, who was reportedly engaged to the granddaughter of Deng Xiaoping, hence giving him an edge in terms of organizing such a big event in the national capital. The two-day festival was held in Chaoyang Park in the eastern part of the city on 10 and 11 September 2007. This was an opportunity for China's indie rock bands to play on the same stage as some of the legendary bands in the history of rock music, including Mark Ramone of the Ramones, the New York Dolls, Public Enemy, Nine Inch Nails, and Cui Jian.

The festival offered two separate stages ensconced in the gently rolling hills of the park. The main stage was surrounded by a fence that cordoned off an area of about 20 meters from the stage. Inside the fence was the VIP section, which gradually filled up with special guests, while the great mass of concert goers stood or sat outside the fence upon the hill. Uniformed guards keep the VIP section free of unwanted guests.

Some men try to climb over the VIP fence at the Beijing Pop Festival held in Chaoyang Park in September 2007, while guards prevent them from crossing over. In the background, Public Enemy performs on stage (photo by Andrew Field)

ANDREW DAVID FIELD

The Beijing Pop Festival ended the rocking summer of 2007 with a glorious global celebration of rock and roll. The festival attracted performers and fans from many countries around the world, showcasing the deep connections of rock music to other forms, styles, and subgenres of music including punk, rap, pop, industrial, techno, and folk—a far wider variety than in the Beijing rock club scene—along with people from other parts of the world. They came together to enjoy the performances, with colorful picnic blankets spread out like on a beach or a park anywhere in the world.

The entrance fee of 200 RMB (250 at the door) reduced the crowd to those who could afford to pay for tickets, but still, hundreds of people attended each day. Local indie rock bands included Hedgehog, the Scoff, and Brain Failure, who were slotted into the early afternoon time slot when the crowd was still gathering. Brain Failure with their lead singer Xiao Rong generated a moshing frenzy among a sizable group of young Chinese and foreign men gathered outside the VIP fence, which I documented while trying to keep my camera from being knocked about and damaged by the whirling bodies. As usual, during the song 'Coming Down to Beijing', the chorus line of 'B.E.I.J.I.N.G.' was echoed by the crowd as they raised their arms and their fists to the music.

Over the duration of the festival, the existence of the VIP area and its surrounding fence became a point of tension. Some people outside the area attempted to climb or air-surf their way across the fence, only to repelled back by the uniformed guards at the perimeter. The energy of the crowd picked up during the New York Dolls concert and the Ramones concert. At one point during the Ramones concert, drummer Marky Ramone announced to the crowd that they needed to calm down if they wished to see another festival in the future.

ROCKING THE CHINESE NATION

A crowd of punk enthusiasts and other fans of rock music raise their fists in unison to the song 'Coming Down to Beijing' performed on stage by Brain Failure during the Beijing Pop Festival in September 2007 (photo by Andrew Field)

Throughout the festival, there were quite a few crowd-surfers, both male and female, foreign and Chinese, who provided extra amusement for the audience. While the VIP boundary area prevented any close interactions with the musicians for the bulk of the audience, at least one band member attempted to close that gap. During the concert of the Japanese rock band Rize, the lead singer and guitarist, who was shirtless, baring his taut body covered with tattoos, jumped off the stage. Guitar in hand, he ran to the edge of the VIP fence to commune and pump fists with the audience members outside the fence, as the guards tried to usher him back to the stage. The crowd-surfing and fence-climbing antics continued during the Cui Jian and Public Enemy shows.

The crowd had calmed down on the second night for the Nine Inch Nails, whose operatic music and riveting performance by lead singer Trent Reznor kept most of the audience captivated. Even so, the Beijing Pop Festival brought out youthful libidinous and rebellious energies that were always threatening to burst out of the containers devised by authorities to keep them in control. This reminded me of what Michael Pettis had to say when I interviewed him in the office of his label Maybe Mars in the fall of 2007:

> China is going through so much change, and such radical change, that it is opening quickly. I think places that are going through major social transformations also tend to be places where people think much more radically about what they're doing and what they expect for the future. They break away from the older constraints, and get thrown in unexpectedly into the new.

His observations made me think of the scenes of moshing, crowd-surfing, and fence-jumping that I witnessed at the Beijing Pop Festival and at other festivals in Shanghai, Beijing, and elsewhere in China over the coming years.

In addition to the Midi Music Festival and the Beijing Pop Festival, another festival started up in 2007, organized by the record company Modern Sky. In the fall of 2007, I attended the first annual Modern Sky Festival held on 2-4 October in Beijing's Haidian Park in the western Haidian District. The festival featured dozens of local rock bands including Re-TROS, Lonely China Day, Joyside, Snapline, Carsick Cars, New Pants, and P.K. 14. The headliner band was the Yeah Yeah Yeahs, an indie rock band from New York featuring lead singer Karen O, who was often compared to SUBS singer Kang Mao in the local media, or vice versa. Despite the rain, which turned the festival grounds to mud, they delivered a fantastic performance to a huge crowd.

As it turned out, the year 2007 marked the apex of rock festivals in Beijing. During and after the Olympic Year of 2008, rock festivals in Beijing would either be cancelled with short notice or else relegated way to the outskirts of the city in satellite towns like Mengtougou and Tongzhou. This golden era of Beijing's openness and tolerance towards rock music, and of its dominance over all other cities in China vis-à-vis rock music, was beginning to draw to a close.

5
KEEPING UP WITH THE BEIJING ROCK SCENE

AT THE END of 2007, I left Beijing and moved to Shanghai, where I have been lived ever since. Over the years, I returned to Beijing periodically to revisit the city's rock clubs and festival scenes. I also attempted to keep up with some of the people whom I identified as key players in those scenes, including club owner Michael Pettis, singer-songwriters Yang Haisong and Kang Mao, record shop owner Lao Yang, and record label owner Matt Kagler, among others. Sadly, I witnessed the demise of the clubs that together constituted the core of the rock scenes in Beijing. Over the next several years, MAO Live House, 2 Kolegas, D-22 and Yugong Yishan eventually all closed down. Yet the city also saw the rise of some new clubs that continued to support the live performances of original rock bands (as opposed to cover bands) in the city. But in the years following my initial foray into the rock scene in 2007, Beijing lost its status as the epicenter of rock in China for a number of reasons that this chapter clarifies.

The development of rock music and other forms of creative cultural expression in China must of course be contextualized within the broader sphere of cultural, political, and social spheres in which they operate. Since I began documenting the rock scenes of China in 2007, China experienced the 2008 Beijing Olympics, which was billed as China's big 'coming out' celebration to the world. It then held the Shanghai World Expo in 2010, which attracted hundreds of thousands of people to Shanghai from all over the world and millions from all over China. Both these major international events contributed to the transformation of those cities in sometimes contradictory ways, opening them up to greater globalization while also subjecting them to government crackdowns on many forms of public expression, including club scenes and bar streets.

Meanwhile, this period also saw the ascension of Xi Jinping to the number one position of leadership over China. This process began in 2007 with his promotion into the Politburo and continued with his appointment to the top position of General Secretary of the CCP and therefore paramount leader of the country in 2012. Xi Jinping quickly established a strong reputation in China and abroad for his campaigns to tighten Party discipline and control the ideological and media spheres in China. These campaigns were partly a product of his own upbringing as the son of a CCP leader, Xi Zhongxun, and arguably a reaction to the 'Jasmine Revolutions' in the Middle East. Regardless of their origins and motivations, these political campaigns also affected the country's art and music scenes, even if the influences were not always entirely transparent. For Beijing, it meant the end of a 'golden period' of art and music in the city, yet for other cities, the rock and roll revolution was just getting started.

The End of Rock Festivals in the National Capital

The festivals that I witnessed in Beijing, Shanghai, and Hunan in 2007 were a positive sign that rock music was on the rise in China and that the gates were opening more widely for a much greater variety of musical sounds, styles, and voices to enter the country. Yet when the Modern Sky Festival was held again in Beijing in 2009, the city government rather suddenly took away the privilege to bring in foreign rock bands. Many surmised that the tipping point for this decision came from an event involving Icelandic rock-pop performer Bjork. During a concert in Shanghai in March 2008, she screamed out to the audience, 'Free Tibet!' thereby causing the Ministry of Culture, which had hitherto been somewhat grudgingly supportive of rock bands coming in from abroad to perform on China's stages, to be more careful about who they let into China's doors and onto its public stages. Significantly, after a successful three-year run, the year 2007 was also the final year for the Beijing Pop Festival. Owing to the 2008 Beijing Olympics and other factors, that festival was discontinued after its triumphal moment in September 2007.

After a long, cold Beijing winter, the May Day holiday is an ideal time for running outdoor music festivals. There were still some festivals taking place in 2011, most notably the Strawberry Music Festival and the Midi Festival. The Strawberry Festival

With her image heroically enlarged on the big screen, Atom, the diminutive drummer of Hedgehog, sings and plays guitar on the stage at the Strawberry Festival in Tongzhou Canal Park in May 2011 before a crowd of thousands (photo by Andrew Field)

was organized by Modern Sky Records, and showcased some of their own bands as well as many international acts. Midi Festival was China's most venerable music festival, having taken place annually in the nation's capital since 1997, with only a few breaks in between. Nevertheless, both festivals were held well outside the city and attending both involved traveling far across the expansive mountain-enclosed plains surrounding Beijing.

The Strawberry Festival was held on the green rolling hills of Tongzhou Canal Park, featuring several stages, and attracting thousands of attendees who purchased tickets either in advance or at the gates. For me, the highlight of the festival was to see the diminutive Atom performing with her band Hedgehog in front of a crowd of thousands, her gigantic image tele-projected onto the hillside around the concert stage. It was good to see Hedgehog doing so well and getting so much recognition since their debut in the Beijing rock clubs in 2007, even if most members of the festival crowd were seeing them for the first and only time. Over the next decade, Hedgehog's name and reputation would continue to grow both in China and abroad.

I also went to see SUBS performing at the Midi Festival. That year, the festival was held well outside of the city, relegated to the Jinglanddao Park in the Mentougou District, at least one hour's drive beyond the western-most part of Beijing. Wind kicked up whirlpools of dust and dirt that seemed to swirl around the performers and their audience in the heat of the spotlights. Even so, the crowd of Chinese and foreigners was quite sizable and dozens of bands representing many different genres of rock music played on several stages in the spacious park. The highlight of the event for me was watching SUBS perform as Kang Mao tried out some new songs as well as some of their 'oldies'. Like Atom at the Strawberry Festival, Kang Mao's performance was projected onto a large screen at the edge of the

After their concert at MIDI Festival in Mengtougou near Beijing in May 2011, SUBS band members pose with the author. Left to right: Li Fan, Andrew Field, Kang Mao, Wu Hao, and Zhu Lei

stage, which allowed the fans to see her wild performance up close. By this time, their drummer Zhang Shun had left the band to raise a family, and they had a new drummer named Li Fan.

Under the new leadership of Xi Jinping, rock festivals continued to operate throughout the Chinese nation after 2012, yet they did so under an increasing amount of scrutiny and restriction by the authorities. As reported in *Vice News* (8 May 2015), a rash of incidents suggested a growing trend of control, at least in the nation's capital. In March 2015, a heavy metal festival called 330 Metal Fest, organized annually since 2002 by Spring and Autumn metal band member Kou Zhengyu, was shut down suddenly after police stormed the Tango club in Beijing where it was being held. That year, the annual Strawberry Music Festival which had operated in Beijing since 2009, was denied a permit to run in Beijing, and the Midi Festival was relegated to the southern city of Suzhou.

ROCKING THE CHINESE NATION

In 2015, a terrible incident on the Bund in Shanghai during the New Year celebration resulted in the deaths of many Chinese tourists after a panicked crowd trampled on them. This added to the tension of hosting and supporting large public events. With heightened restrictions (all bands and lyrics for these festivals now needed approval from the Ministry of Culture) and a growing sense of paranoia, local officials and police often intervened to prevent any possibility of coming under the severe scrutiny of the CCP leadership. As reported by *The Economist*, covering the same trends ('Mosh No More,' 9 May 2015), Xi Jinping himself announced that art in China should 'embody socialist core values' and represent the culture and will of 'the people' in China. It is doubtful that headbanging to metal bands or moshing to punk bands in a crowded club in Beijing is what China's great leader meant by this statement. This may help explain why, since 2015, the nation's capital has virtually ceased to host large rock festivals, letting them flourish in more remote parts of the country. Under various pressures, described in the next section, many of the city's veteran rock clubs also shut down.

Saying Goodbye to Old Friends and Clubs in the Beijing Rock Scene

Over the years, I continued to touch base with at least some of the musicians and rock promoters I had interviewed in 2007. The overall trend that I discerned from repeated visits, follow-up interviews, and news items from Beijing was that the rock scene I had documented went through a period of flourishing, development, and differentiation between 2008 and 2011, followed by a rather precipitous decline after 2012. While stalwarts such as Michael Pettis and Yang Haisong continued to carve out a niche for themselves and for indie rock in the city, many other promoters, bands, and clubs disappeared from the scene.

Among the casualties was Matt Kagler's label, Tag Team Records. I last saw Matt in 2009, when he was still operating his company and was still somewhat upbeat about the rock scenes in China. A year later, he mysteriously shuttered his company and left an angry 'Why I left Beijing' message online (chinamusicradar. com, 17 December 2010). His message highlighted his quixotic efforts to keep it 'indie' and not go the route of commercializing the music for the sake of a quick buck:

> As much as I hate to say it, I completely lost interest in the Chinese scene and therefore bowed out. It wasn't as much a monetary decision as much as it was as informed thing. I mean, Tag Team most certainly couldn't keep up with the pocket books of Michael Pettis and Shen over at Modern [Sky], but we WERE trying to do things as "indie" as possible and that doesn't fly in the land of Zippo Nights and Converse whatnots. We were uninterested in those kind of things per say and therefore threw the towel in.

By this time, global fashion companies like Converse, Dickies, Vans, and other youth-oriented fashion producers had gotten wind of the Chinese indie rock scene and were making inroads into it, paying bands to pose for ads while wearing their products, and sponsoring some of the larger festivals like the Strawberry Festival.

Matt Kagler's online rant reflected the underlying struggle over authenticity among bands, labels, fans, enthusiasts, and supporters of the indie music scene in China. This was no different to any other part of the world where forms and styles of music are heavily contested, and sanctified territories formed, guarded, invaded and conquered with the written word. For some rockers, authenticity lies in not going over to the 'dark side' of commercializing one's music. Over the next few years, I made a few attempts to locate Matt Kagler and connect back with him, but to no avail. It was sad to see him make such a hasty departure from the Beijing rock scene only a year later, especially after producing so many high-quality albums with Lonely China Day and other indie bands in Beijing. Even so, the indie rock scene and other music scenes in Beijing moved on to other labels and other venues.

When I visited Beijing in May 2011 to attend the Midi and Strawberry festivals, I also caught up with Lao Yang, the Sugar Jar record shop owner. Sadly, I discovered that the Sugar Jar was no longer where it once stood in the alleyway a few doors down from the Galleria Continua. The 798 Art Zone was still going strong, and it was thronged with tourists as usual, but there was no sign of the record shop nor of Lao Yang.

Later that week, through some other contacts, I learned that Lao Yang had moved to the art village of Songzhuang on outskirts of eastern Beijing . I paid him a brief visit and found him living in a scene of dry, desert-like starkness that reminded me of New Mexico. He was growing his own vegetables in a tiny garden patch and seemed to be healthy and in good spirits. Nevertheless, Lao Yang told me that his shop had been forcibly shut down after he became involved for a time in a group that proposed making some basic changes to China's system.

An Interview with Michael Pettis at the XP Club in 2015

In 2015, I traveled again to Beijing to catch up with some of the folks I knew from the city's indie rock scene and find out in which directions they had gone in the past few years. My first stop was a small, out-of-the-way rock club in an ancient neighborhood near Houhai in the middle of the city, the XP Club on Di'anmen Road, a couple hundred meters west from the southern entrance to Nanluoguxiang.

'The legend is going to be twenty or thirty years from now that it all started at D-22 in 2005-2008,' Michael Pettis said as I chatted with him in the small office of Maybe Mars Records located in the loft area above the XP Club. 'Which is a bit of an exaggeration,' he admitted, laughing and shrugging, 'but you know, what the hell.' Though handsome as always, he looked older and also thinner than when I first met him in 2007, his gaunt features lit up eerily in the light of his computer screen. I asked about the roles of two other clubs I followed back in 2007, 2 Kolegas and MAO Livehouse, in pushing the indie rock scene.

'What we [D-22] were really famous for was identifying the bands that were going to be the really great bands,' he said, rather than just featuring musician friends or already well-established bands. He pointed out that D-22 discovered the band Hedgehog.

I asked him why D-22 had closed in 2012, and he replied that he had been 'getting bored' with the club, which had become too popular and was attracting the drop-in 'backpacker' crowd. He wanted to set up a club that was even more experimental and cutting edge, so he started XP. Opened in late 2012, XP was meant to be an insider musicians' scene. According to Michael, bands like Carsick Cars, who had since become very famous in the Chinese indie scene and internationally as well, could not even play at the club unless they did so without any advance notice, since they tended to draw in such a huge crowd that it overtaxed the venue's size. 'D-22 could get 400 people but this place comfortably max out at 100,' he said. 'I wanted to get a place that was small enough that I could really focus on the experimental and not have to worry about filling the club.'

ROCKING THE CHINESE NATION

One of the events that drove the experimental side of XP was called Zoomin' Night. This was a curated event every Tuesday night that attracted some of the city's more adventurous musicians. According to Josh Feola, a commentator on Chinese indie rock scenes, the title came from a P.K. 14 song called 'Zaomianye'. It was curated by Zhu Wenbo, a former veterinarian who had turned his passions to music. It started at D-22 in 2009 and later carried over to XP and became a fixture of the club's offerings.

I asked Michael how these sorts of experimental music events at XP had influenced more 'conventional' indie rock bands in the scene. Chui Wan and Birdstriking were two newer bands in the Maybe Mars pantheon that Michael said were now the bands to watch in the indie scene, and he told me that they had been influenced by some of the avant-garde performances of Zoomin' Night.

As it turned out, Chui Wan was performing the following night at Yugong Yishan, which in 2015 was still in the same location just a few hundred meters east of XP club. I asked Michael whether he thought that the Chinese rock bands he was promoting would eventually become famous worldwide, and he replied, 'Famous in what sense? In the sense that Sonic Youth is famous?'

I agreed that that was a good standard to apply, since everyone who knew indie music would know that band.

'As soon as we can get one of our bands to play Saturday Night Live or, I guess not Letterman anymore but one of those things,' he replied, citing two popular American TV shows famous for showcasing new rock acts.

One of the bands that Michael had promoted vigorously since their breakout on the scene in 2007 was Carsick Cars. During our interview, he proudly pointed out that since their first concert tour in Vienna and Prague with Sonic Youth in August 2007, Zhang Shouwang and his band, whose lineup changed frequently over the years, had already established themselves internationally and that they were playing the biggest concert festival in Europe that year, and also Midem in Cannes, France. They also had gigs in Lyon and in Utrecht in Eindhoven in the Netherlands, before they returned to Paris perform at L'International.

Kang Mao and SUBS at Temple Bar (5 June 2015)
While many independent bands in China had long since gone over to the 'dark side' of signing contracts with record labels and working with international rock promoters to build their brand, others fiercely guarded their own musical and financial independence. One of those bands was SUBS. Over the years, I kept up with Kang Mao and touched base with her many times during my occasional visits back to Beijing. As I describe in the next chapter, I also saw several performances of the band at different venues in Shanghai, where they never failed to draw in a moshing crowd. SUBS continued to book their own gigs, produce and sell their own independent record albums, and chart their own musical course. Other band members came and went. Zhang Shun left the band around 2011 to raise a family back in Wuhan. Bassist Zhu Lei eventually departed as well, leaving core band members Kang Mao and Wu Hao. In 2012, they were joined briefly by an Australian drummer named Carl Edmunds, who performed with them for a year or so. American drummer Josh Feola joined the band in 2014 and as of 2017 he was still with the band, which was touring actively around China. Eventually, he moved on and the band acquired yet another drummer.

On Friday, 5 June 2015, I texted Kang Mao and was delighted to learn she planned to be at a venue called Temple Bar later that evening. The bar was located across the road from the MAO

Live House near the northern entrance of Nanluoguxiang. It was on the second floor of a building that housed a restaurant and another music bar called Dada, founded by Michael Ohlsson. The concert that evening was organized and emceed by Darryl Lyle, a flamboyant American promoter of the underground punk rock scene in China, who ran a festival called Drunk Fest of which this was a part. The second part of the festival took place the following day in Tongzhou.

That night, the lineup in this club began with two bands composed largely of foreigners: Cut Frenzy from Harbin and Nakoma from Beijing. They were followed by a veteran band of the Chinese punk rock scene, Demerit, whose members played a vigorous set to a crowd of around 100 people. Beijing had just passed a law forbidding smoking in bars and restaurants, so all the smokers had to go outside to do their thing. I caught up with Kang Mao outside the club where all the smokers congregated, and met their new drummer, Josh Feola.

Finally, well after midnight, in a word-of-mouth performance that went completely unadvertised, SUBS was the last band to play. Accompanied by Wu Hao on guitar, and with Josh Feola backing them on drums, Kang Mao sang as she played a small electronic keyboard. In the tiny venue, her performance seemed more toned-down than other times I had seen her perform. It seemed her style was maturing, and the raw punk feel of SUBS back in 2007 had been replaced by something more subdued. They were playing some of their latest songs, which were still edgy and powerful and managed to get the somewhat diminished late night crowd roiling.

Seeing Yang Haisong and Chui Wan at Yugong Yishan (6 June 2015)

Another person whom I intended to catch up in 2015 with was

Yang Haisong. We arranged to meet at the rock club Yugong Yishan prior to a concert by Chui Wan, one of the front runners on the Maybe Mars label. The label had by then produced over 60 albums from indie bands all over China. After leaving the label for a while and then being wooed back by Michael Pettis, Yang Haisong produced many of them. He was very proud of the bands he helped to gain local if not global prominence, including Chui Wan, whose concert was being held that night to celebrate their latest album produced on the Maybe Mars label. In his conversation with me, he corroborated Michael's observations that the indie rock scene in China had greatly expanded and that there were now great Chinese indie bands playing in cities all over the country. Recently, he had been working with a band from the city of Chengdu in Sichuan Province to produce their album.

Later that evening, we caught the Chui Wan concert along with around 600 other guests in a tightly packed crowd at Yugong Yishan. The band consisted of bassist Wu Qiong, guitarist Liu Xinyu, vocalist/instrumentalist Yan Yulong, and drummer Li Zichao. They were reputed to have a Middle Eastern sound influenced by Sufi music, and indeed their songs were rhythmic and hypnotic and largely instrumental, heavy on keyboards and synthesized sounds. That night, female bassist Wu Qiong was wearing a purple robe and her hair was done in a tidy bowl cut making her look like an Oriental priestess of post-punk rock. She contributed to the vocalized chants that accompanied some of their songs. The effect was strange, enchanting, and cultish. The experience was akin to having stumbled onto some ancient ceremonial performance held secretly in the deep recesses of an Egyptian pyramid as the Pharoah's remains are embalmed and mummified in preparation for the afterlife. Certainly, the performance by Chui Wan was an indication that even in the wake of the closing of some of Beijing's best rock clubs, China's indie music scene was continuing to develop in new and unprecedented directions.

School Bar: A Small Yet Welcome New Addition to Beijing's Rock Club Scene

Another rock club that arose during the 2010s was School Bar. This small club was nestled in a commercialized hutong neighborhood located just west of the Lama Temple (雍和宫) in the middle of Beijing. School Bar was a tiny venue, with a small stage and room for only a few dozen customers at most, and this is being charitable. I first visited the club in June 2015 and caught the performance of a female Asian American punk rocker. At the time of my visit, it was hard for me to imagine this club carrying on the torch of indie rock music after the run of great venues like MAO Livehouse, D-22, and 2 Kolegas.

Even so, following the closure of these clubs, School Bar helped to sustain the diminishing live rock scene in Beijing. Liu Hao, the bassist for Beijing punk band Joyside, was one of the co-founders. After the band split up in 2009, citing artistic differences (they later reformed the band), he joined together with another musician named Liu Fei to start this club in Wudaoyong Hutong. As for Bian Yuan, the Jim Morrison-esque singer who fronted what is still considered one of Beijing's greatest underground punk bands, he was known to hang out at School Bar with his ex-band mate and indulge his habit of heavy drinking. In April 2014, he reportedly launched a solo album there called *Dead Inside*, which was inspired by listening to a lot of Brian Eno and looking out at night at the stars while contemplating the vastness and emptiness of space.

ANDREW DAVID FIELD

The End of an Era: Beijing Rock Club Crackdowns, Closings, and Transformations

During my interview with Michael Pettis in June 2015, he told me that club XP was slated to close in July. The Maybe Mars outfit was moving to another location nearby and could not afford to keep the venue. Michael planned to use his new venue instead to showcase some Chinese visual artists. In April the following year, MAO Live House also closed, reportedly due to the rising cost of rent in Beijing. SUBS were given the honor of being the last band to perform there. A Reuters report referenced owner Li Chi who said that it 'was forced to close due to tighter rules on live performances and rising rent.' Another source quoted in the article cited the competition of discos and nightclubs as another reason why rock clubs were suffering in the national capital.

The club 2 Kolegas was shut down around that time reportedly after a government crackdown on drugs which led to a police raid on the club, during which they closed with all patrons inside and all required to submit to a urine test, resulting in the arrest of four Chinese and five foreigners presumably for drug use. According to the report, the foreigners were deported from the country. Meanwhile, most if not all the glorious outdoor rock festivals that once graced the city had disappeared or moved to other parts of China.

Another noisy departure from the Beijing rock scene was Kaiser Kuo. In late 2015, he publicly announced that he was leaving his job with Baidu, China's most prominent internet company, for whom he had served as a spokesperson for many years. After more than twenty years of living in China's grungy rock capital and rocking the country with his bands Tang Dynasty, Spring & Autumn, Dirty Deeds and other rock bands, he was moving with his family back to the USA. On 31 May, 2016, he performed his last concert with the band Spring & Autumn at

Yugong Yishan along with the band's former lead singer Yang Meng, who returned to Beijing specially for the occasion from his home in Yunnan. Kaiser's departure was one example of a much larger exodus from Beijing of international families, who were increasingly concerned with the shocking levels of air pollution in the city, among other things.

As of 2017, there were still a few active rock clubs in Beijing, including Yugong Yishan and School Bar. These were the last holdouts of the diminishing Beijing rock club scene, which had experienced its golden era ten years or so ago. Eventually, Yugong Yishan and Temple Bar closed. As of 2022, all that remained of those clubs was School Bar. It appears that the tightening of government regulations and restrictions on live performance venues, coupled with rising rents, exoduses due to air pollution, and the rising popularity of clubs featuring electronic dance music were all nails in the coffin of rock music in Beijing. Meanwhile, the rock scene that had once centered itself in Beijing continued to spread deeper into other cities in China, drawing youths in far more cities and towns than ever before into China's rock scenes. One of those cities was Shanghai.

6

STEPPING OUT FROM BEIJING'S SHADOW: THE EVOLVING ROCK SCENES IN SHANGHAI

WHILE BEIJING remained the rock capital of China into the 2010s, Shanghai was striving to develop its own identity as a Chinese rock and roll city. To be sure, the primary musical identity of Shanghai, at least for the international and tourist crowd, was as a city of jazz. This goes back to the 'golden age' of the 1930s, when Shanghai was the undisputed jazz capital of Asia. Since the 1990s, several jazz and blues clubs had sprung up in the city, notably the House of Blues and Jazz, the Cotton Club, and a few years later, the JZ Club, all of which offered live jazz music performed by Chinese and foreign musicians from all over the world.

The 2000s also saw the rise of several new rock clubs and festivals in the city, some of which persisted into the 2020s. Most others rose and fell quickly. Yet Shanghai managed to maintain the sparks of a culture of original and inventive live rock music going throughout this era. While rock bands coming down from Beijing were at least partly responsible for sustaining the live scenes in Shanghai, the city produced many inventive and original rock bands of its own and became a regional lodestone for rock musicians from all over China to test their metal against some of the best bands in the country.

ROCKING THE CHINESE NATION

(1) Ark Live House in Xintiandi; (2) Original Tanghui Bar on Xingfu Road;
(3) Tanghui Bar on 85 Huating Road; (4) 4 Live on 8 Jianguo Zhong Road (No. 8 Bridge);
(5) Harley's Bar or Harley's Underground on 265 Nandan Road;
(6) Zhijiang Dream Factory on 28 Yuyao Road (Tonglefang); (7) Yuyintang on 851 Kaixuan Road;
(8) Windows Underground on 698 Nanjing West Road; (9) Original Mao Livehouse in Red Town;
(10) Mao Livehouse on 308 Chongqing Nan Road; (11) Inferno Bar on 658 Dapu Road

A Crash Course in Chinese Indie Rock: The Rock It Festival in Shanghai (29 June to 1 July 2007)

In a country as large and diverse as China, it is always difficult to assess the total number of rock bands active nationally. As of 2007, there were purportedly several hundred bands in Beijing alone, and hundreds of others in other provinces and cities, and numbers were growing year by year. While Cui Jian's Concert on the Sands in Hunan Province provided me with a unique opportunity to see Chinese rock bands performing to a large and semi-rural audience in China's heartland, my first opportunity to witness the sheer variety of styles of rock bands in China was a three-day rock festival in Shanghai, dubbed 'Rock It!'. Featuring 36 bands, or roughly twelve per day, this festival took place in

Wu Jun, the organizer of the Rock It Festival held at Dino Beach Water Park in Shanghai in June 2007, on the site of the festival grounds (photo by Andrew Field)

the Dino Beach Water Park in the southern Minhang District of Shanghai. When I arrived on the drizzly afternoon of 29 June, a crew was busy erecting the stage on an artificial sand beach fronting an artificial wave pool, where people were lazing about on the water on yellow inflatable rafts shaped like huge doughnuts.

The organizer of the festival was a tall, crew-cut Shanghainese rock musician named Wu Jun. He told me that he had tapped into his own personal network of rock bands to organize this festival.

'I put together this festival to expose rock music to a wider audience in Shanghai, including many people who have never seen rock music performed live before,' he said, adding that around 400 people turned up on the first day (a rainy day) and 1,500 on the second. The crowd was small at the start of the concert in the early afternoon and seemed to be composed of mainly rock musicians and their groupies or fans as well as reporters from the local media, but it picked up steadily over the day. By late afternoon the crowd included curious older people, no doubt including moms and dads, a few grandparents, and plenty of youngsters of all ages, though most were obviously there for the water pool. Even so, people brought their water floats onto the beach to use as seats and enjoy the show, and many younger people danced in front of the stage in swimsuits and bikinis, giving it the flavor of a beach party. By evening, the area of the beach fronting the stage was packed full of young Chinese and foreigners who had come to see the headlining acts.

The festival was my first glimpse into the sheer size and variety of the rock scene in China. Wu Jun said more than half of the bands were based in Shanghai, although many were composed of musicians who had come to live and play in the city from elsewhere in China. There were also around ten bands from Beijing. The rest hailed from many cities across the country, notably including the port city of Dalian, and the western cities of Chongqing and Kunming. Almost all the players were Chinese. Each band performed for around thirty minutes before the next band mounted the stage for their sound check.

Among the various genres and subgenres of musical styles represented, I detected metal (heavy, death, thrash, goth — you name it!), punk, hardcore, reggae, hip-hop, new wave, Britpop, grunge, and funk. There were also some folk bands with regional Chinese influences and even some using traditional Chinese instruments. Examples of the latter included Mountain Men (山人) from Yunnan Province, as well as Pow-wow (巫师来了) from Chongqing. Both bands generated a huge buzz among the crowd.

Shanghai's own top rock acts were showcased, including veteran band Crystal Butterfly, as well as newer bands such as the Honeys, Banana Monkey, Crazy Mushroom, and Flying Fruit (羽果). Crystal Butterfly and Flying Fruit, a band originally hailing from Jiangxi Province, seemed to lean more towards a

Britpop sound, with echoey guitar work somewhat reminiscent of U2. Others like Crazy Mushroom, a funky band led by a male singer with a Mohawk, mixed rap, hip-hop and grungy rock together into a mishmash. Crazy Mushroom's act ended in a big call-and-response session which energized the crowd to a cover of 'What's Up' by 4 Non-Blondes: 'I say hey, what's going on!' They seemed quite popular with their Shanghai fan base. Banana Monkey was a blues-inflected garage band with a retro '60s feel to it, fronted by a Chinese singer who went by the name of Bono. They were also one of the highlights of the festival. Beijing bands featured in the concert included Hedgehog, Joyside, and the New Pants, whose crazy antics include the keyboardist removing his pants onstage, revealing a flowery white one-piece bodysuit, and throwing himself into the audience.

The festival ended on Sunday night with a performance by the Beijing band Re-TROS. Their music was somewhat lugubrious, but also catchy, humorous, and fun. Songs like 'Laugh from the

People use inflatable water rafts to sit on the beach as they watch a band perform during the Shanghai Rock It Festival in June 2007 (photo by Andrew Field)

Time' from their 2005 album *Cut-Off* distributed on the Modern Sky label and on Tag Team Records, captured a dark sound like that of the British bands Bauhaus and Joy Division. Re-TROS cofounders Hua Dong (male, lead vocalist and guitarist) and Liu Min (female, bassist) openly acknowledged these two British '80s industrial bands as their key influences. Their music had a gothic vibe to it. Bassist Liu Min's high ethereal voice provided a counterpart to the voice of lead singer Hua Dong as he sang a song that reminded the listeners that they would soon enough be old and dead. Onstage there was an intensity to Hua Dong's performance, both on guitar and on vocals, that was indeed reminiscent of Joy Division's lead singer Ian Curtis, and it was not surprising that this Beijing band was chosen by Wu Jun to end the festival, signifying the dominance of Beijing bands even in a Shanghai-based music festival. This was the final year the Rock It Festival was held, but Shanghai continued to see the rise of music festivals focused on rock and roll, including the Strawberry Festival, the Yue Festival, and many others.

An Interview with Shanghai Rock Promoter Wu Jun

Wu Jun, the organizer of the Rock It Festival, was a Shanghainese musician, who like many other promoters of rock music in China had been active in the rock scene for many years. When I interviewed him in 2007 after attending the festival, he was running a recording studio called 13D (the apartment number), located in a residential apartment in Shanghai's Xuhui District. The studio was full of instruments and equipment and featured a soundproofed room. He told me his studio had been running for two years, and that the rock scene in Shanghai was really starting to pick up: "Over the past two years or so I've seen the rise of an atmosphere far more conducive to the growth of indie rock. It's getting better and better here in Shanghai. There are more places to perform, and more opportunities. It used to be that a rock band might only have four or five opportunities in a year to perform. Now it's more like four or five opportunities per month."

He said the culture of Shanghai was not very supportive of rock music, and mentioned the predominance of karaoke halls, where guests performed songs in private rooms with friends to Cantopop and Mandopop soundtracks. Sure, there were plenty of kids playing instruments in the city, but they were mostly playing pianos.

'If parents in Shanghai buy their kid an instrument, it's usually a piano,' he sighed, leaning back on his couch. 'They're willing to put down 10,000 *yuan* for a piano—but if a kid asks them for 10,000 *yuan* to buy a nice guitar, that's another story entirely!'

The piano signified a kind of prestige, refinement, and social status that the guitar did not. Despite the rise of rock clubs and bands in Shanghai, Wu Jun's comment reflected the limitations of rock music's spread in the city. This was perhaps one reason why Shanghai attracted far fewer rock bands than Beijing. If a band from the provinces like SUBS wished to achieve their rock'n'roll dream, it was Beijing and not Shanghai, where they made their home. At least, such was the case in 2007.

The Limitations of the Shanghai Rock Scene: An Interview with Michael Ohlsson in 2007

During one of my many visits from Beijing to Shanghai in the summer of 2007, I arranged an interview with Michael Ohlsson, an American DJ and club entrepreneur. At the time, he was helping to book bands for a new rock club called 4 Live. His big claim to fame was that in 2009 he founded a bar and lounge club called Dada on Xingfu Road in Shanghai offering an eclectic range of music, and three years later opened a Dada club in

Beijing as well. At the time of my first interview with him in 2007, Michael was working for Split Works, a Shanghai-based music company run by an Englishman named Archie Hamilton, which was dedicated to bringing music acts from abroad to perform in China. Michael also ran a regular DJ party event held in various clubs around town called Antidote. During the interview, I asked Michael what he thought of the live music scene in Shanghai. Here is what he had to say:

> Well, it's different in Shanghai than it is in other cities. Beijing obviously is the most dynamic rock scene, as far as variety. You can go out every night in Beijing. Even if it's a small gig, you can see some live music. In Shanghai, it's probably once a week you can find live rock music. And there aren't that many bands. Take 4 Live for example, which has been for the last year the premier, and probably the only live rock venue in town. Even there, we had a really hard time finding bands to play, and we were recycling a lot of bands. Bands would play every week, or twice a month. It's just depressing, when we'd look around for more talent in Shanghai. Once or twice a month, we'd fly down a band from Beijing. That's what you had to do.

To further his point, Michael told a story about the money paid and arrangements made for bands coming from Beijing to perform. This story is about SUBS:

> Like 4 Live for example, it would be like 200 [*yuan*] per musician. So, if it's a 4-piece band, 800 *yuan* for a night. Unless it was like a real big act from Beijing that was coming down, like Brain Failure or SUBS or New

> Pants. But there was a bit of a controversy with one of the SUBS shows that we booked, because another promoter in town had also booked SUBS previously and he was angry because they thought that we were paying them too much, and that we were actually going to fly them down instead of putting them on the overnight train. They said it's not good for the scene. Like 'don't spoil these bands', because next time they'll expect us to pay them that much, and we'll never get them to play. The other bands are going to say, 'that's not fair, we want to get paid that much too.' I can understand where they're coming from, but on the other hand, why should they have to ride the 3rd-class train just because they're in a rock band? Are they going to continue doing that?

Clearly the fact that clubs had to pay more money to bring Beijing bands down to Shanghai, whether by train or by plane, served as a serious limiting factor to the growth of the city's rock club scene.

Rock Clubs in Shanghai in the Late 1990s and Early 2000s
While Shanghai boasted many successful live music clubs, the most established ones tended to focus on jazz and blues, not on rock music. I have been studying the club scene in Shanghai since I first lived in the city in the late 1990s. Still, I do not personally recall visiting any rock clubs from that period. Jeroen de Kloet claims the only club in the city where rock music was regularly performed was a gritty, student-oriented club called Tribesman located near Fudan University in Yangpu district, and the club did channel the spirit of the Beijing underground rock scene. This district is far away from the city center, and its clubs have always

been marginal to the life of the city. Yet like Wudaokou in Beijing, the district had the potential to shape the tastes of generations of elite university students at nearby Fudan and other universities in Shanghai. But in the more commercialized and fashionable environment of Shanghai, the neighborhood never succeeded in producing a sustained and influential rock club scene.

In my own personal recollection, the first rock clubs arose in or near the center of the city in the early 2000s. Xintiandi or 'New Heaven and Earth,' a tourist area in the former French Concession area, created out of a reconstructed neighborhood of old-style row-houses, opened in 2001. Soon afterward, this glitzy entertainment and leisure zone became thronged with hordes of tourists and locals hopping among a wide selection of fancy clubs, restaurants, and bars. One of the early clubs there was Ark Live House, which was a cavernous hall with a balcony looking down on the stage. The club featured local Chinese rock bands, including the Shanghai bands Crystal Butterfly and Cold Fairyland. With its pricey drinks and its central location in a major tourist zone, the club did not attract a youthful rock crowd, at least not one comparable in any way to those of Beijing. It lasted until 2008, and was replaced by another live venue called Brown Sugar. That club focused on funk and soul cover bands playing music from the 1960s and 1970s. While Xintiandi continued to offer live music acts, no other rock club to my knowledge sprouted up there since the short-lived experiment of Ark Live House.

Another early experiment was a live music club called Tang Hui on Xingfu Road, a short road in the Xuhui district that had once been locally famous among hipsters under the name D.D's. Opened by a Chinese rock musician who called himself Zooma, this tiny club did not last very long; it was shut down in 2005, presumably owing to noise complaints from nearby residents.

Which highlights a problem that Shanghai rock and other live music clubs have often faced in Shanghai since at least the 1920s. It is hard in this crowded city to find locations that are not close to residential neighborhoods.

But Zooma reopened Tang Hui even closer to the heart of the city, in a house on Huating Road near Huaihai Road, one of the main thoroughfares running through the former French Concession. It attracted a fair number of foreigners, and featured performances by both local rock bands and imported ones. Nevertheless, again owing to noise complaints from neighbors, as well as the dearth of local talent, the club did not last more than a year or so.

Yet another underground club in Xujiahui at the western edge of the former French Concession was Harley's Bar, a grungy basement club featuring live music that has been operating continuously since 2005. Situated in a densely packed commercial zone, the club has so far survived. In March 2017, among a mixed crowd of Chinese and foreigners, I caught a loud and lively concert there of the expat punk-core band Round Eye, followed by a Thai funk-electronic band called Wasabi Bytes featuring guest artist Afrika Islam, one of the pioneers of hip-hop in 1980s New York.

The Scene at 4 Live Club in 2007
In 2007, while making frequent trips to Shanghai from Beijing, I spent some time at 4 Live, the club where Michael Ohlsson helped to book bands. It was in the 'No. 8 Bridge' (八号桥) zone located on the corner of Jianguo Road and Chongqing South Road, not far from a lively tourist neighborhood known as Tianzifang, and it occupied a spot formerly housing a disco club called La Fabrique. On my first visit to 4 Live on a hot night on 21 July, 2007, I saw two Shanghai bands that had appeared in the

Rock It Festival the previous month: Crazy Mushroom and 45. The former was an eclectic blend of rap, hip hop, pop, and rock fronted by a Chinese guy in a Mohawk hairdo, while the latter was straight-up death metal fronted by a lithe, shirtless Chinese male singer (bellower really) with a goatee, surrounded by dry ice smoke and red lighting, who looked like Asmodeus rising out of a crack in the earth. Both bands delivered great performances that night despite a small audience, but it left me skeptical about the future of this club and of the rock scene in Shanghai.

Another band I saw perform at 4 Live was SUBS, who played there on 26 August 2007. This time, the club had a packed crowd of around 250 people jammed into the main hall and balconies overlooking the stage. The crowd was probably 75 percent foreigners, which was quite different to the Beijing scene where there was usually a more equal mixture (though as mentioned, foreigners tended to predominate in the later hours). Still there were plenty of Chinese rock enthusiasts as well, gathered close to the edge of the stage watching Kang Mao and the band perform. There was a great deal of frenzied moshing going on near the front of the stage, which looked somewhat more violent and aggressive than what I had witnessed in Beijing, with more arm-pushing and fist-pumping. Leading the charge was Dan Shapiro, a young American punk rock musician living in Shanghai, whom I had met at the Rock It Festival the previous month. He was in the middle of the mosh pit, flailing his arms about and pumping his left arm up and down with the music. From the balcony above, I could see his distinctive shiny bald pate and handlebar mustache.

During her performance, Kang Mao went to the edge of the stage several times as she always did to connect better with the crowd, and between songs she gave short impromptu speeches. On this night, her hair hung over her face, shielding her eyes from the audience. In addition to her getup of a tight black leather skirt and white tank top, she was wearing a black tie, loosely draped around her neck. Her hips swayed sexily as she rocked back and forth, taunting the crowd, which was largely male and white. At the front of the hall, near the center of the crowd, stood a very tall Chinese man whose upper body was bare, showing off his taut, muscular body. He seemed to be guarding her from the advances of the foreign men around him, but he was just trying to stand still as they pushed and shoved each other in the mosh pit.

There was a primitive and orgiastic, violence-laden sexuality to this night's performance of Kang Mao. This was enhanced by the liberal use of dry ice to create a fog that enveloped the band, who were lit up in red by the spotlights. Towards the end of the concert, the women in the audience gathered round the stage like acolytes in some strange pagan ritual. Kang Mao taunted them as well, planting her Converse-clad foot atop the amp in front of the stage to show off her bare leg, and getting so close to one blonde-haired girl that she could just about kiss her. The women screamed in delight and awe at this dominant woman shouting and yelling and prancing about on stage. This was not the first time I witnessed this sort of visceral reaction by women to Kang Mao's onstage persona, and not the last time either.

After the concert, I headed outside to get some fresh air and caught up with Dan Shapiro, who was enjoying a smoke. He was all sweaty and glistening after all the moshing. He was wearing a dark jean jacket with the arms cut off, and beneath that was a grey tank top soaked in sweat. A long necklace with jade pendants hangs down his chest.

'What do you think about the band SUBS?' I asked.

'They're a unique band for sure," he replied. 'There's nothing else like that shit in China. It's like an explosion of energy. It's genuine, like there's a lot of pent-up aggression going on there.

You can pick out their influences, but the spirit and the nature of SUBS is original. You'll see punk, you'll see metal, you'll see rock'n'roll, but this is sort of like a mixture of all of that. All of them are great players, and they put on a great show. I would say it's the best band in China going right now.'

Clearly SUBS had a strong reputation among rock enthusiasts, and they were able to draw a full house to an otherwise defunct rock club in Shanghai. After the concert was over, Kang Mao and Wu Hao set up at a table outside the club, selling their CDs and t-shirts to a long line of fans. A few months later, the club folded.

Zhijiang Dream Factory

Despite what Michael Ohlsson had to say about the scene in Shanghai, 4 Live was not the only rock club in town. One of the first clubs I visited in Shanghai in the summer of 2007 was Zhijiang Dream Factory, which Rock It Festival organizer Wu Jun recommended to me. Housed in the top floor of a cavernous, echoey old factory warehouse on Yuyao Road in the middle of the Jing'an District, with a capacity of up to 800 guests, and located just down the road from one of the most successful nightclubs in town called Muse, this was an up-and-coming live music venue that attracted some big crowds and plenty of small ones.

A year later, in November 2008, I saw SUBS perform there, generating the usual wild whirligig of energy as they played to a deeply engaged crowd. In 2009, along with around 1,000 other people, I was delighted to catch American indie folk musician Andrew Bird performing there, brought to China courtesy of Archie Hamilton's company Split Works. Nevertheless, the focus of the club was to showcase local Shanghai bands and other Chinese rock bands, and the audience for that was not big enough or regular enough to be sustainable. The club lasted another year and then shut down, presumably because

People heading into the rock club Yuyintang in Shanghai in July 2016. By this time the club was sponsored by Absolut Vodka (photo by Andrew Field)

the venue's owners could not cover costs (and reportedly, the building's management took all the sales from alcohol).

Yuyintang: Shanghai's Most Sustained and Eclectic Rock Club Scene

Shanghai's rock scene was not as dynamic or influential as Beijing's. Yet despite the tendency of clubs to come and go, the city did manage to sustain a few solid rock clubs over the years. One was Yuyintang 育音堂, a club that reminded me in some ways of 2 Kolegas in Beijing. It was located on Kaixuan Road just north of Yan'an West Road, a large and busy street in the western part of Changning District, with an elevated subway line running along it, right across from one of the stations. Founded by Zhang Haisheng, a Shanghainese rock musician in 2004 and moved to its current location near Tianshan Park in 2008, this was the most longstanding if not the most outstanding rock club in the city. One key to its longevity is that the park is located right behind the club, so noise is not as big an issue since there were no immediate neighbors to disturb.

Anybody who has spent as much time studying club scenes in Shanghai as I have will understand that space is a paramount issue in the city, whose population is clustered in multi-storied residential districts particularly in the heart of the city. Since the 1990s, the city has experienced both a huge population expansion and a massive building boom, bringing it up to its current status as one of the world's largest mega-cities. If you do the math, you can easily determine that the population density of Shanghai is around four times that of Beijing. This both raises the price of real estate and makes it difficult for music clubs to operate without disturbing surrounding residents.

Club owners in Shanghai have long since figured out that placing your club in a park gives it a longer life if you can work out the *guanxi* (relationship) with the local authorities to do so. This was true of the famed Park 97, a club located in Fuxing Park that at its peak in the early 2000s was raking in more money and bringing in more A-list DJs than any other in Shanghai, if not in all of China. At Yuyintang, patrons could spill out into the park, hang out there and smoke, quaff a beer, chat with their mates, make out, play Frisbee in the summer months, or chill (figuratively if not literally) in the winter months. There were no neighbors around to complain about the noise or the drunken antics of the customers. Inside, the club was small and tight, with a 5-square meter floor for the audience to stand or dance or just squeeze onto as the musicians play on the stage. It comfortably accommodated around 150 people. I saw quite a few concerts over the years at Yuyintang featuring bands from Shanghai, Beijing, other cities in China, and abroad—not only rock music, but also folk and jazz as well.

One local performer who played regularly at Yuyintang and at many other live music venues in town was a shaggy, long-haired Shanghainese musician named Zhou Chao. An accomplished and highly original guitarist, he usually performed solo. He could play a wide range of styles, sometimes favoring a more folk style on acoustic guitar, and other times jamming on the electric guitar. He had a very original style of playing that had some Chinese roots to it, reminding me in a way of the Yunnanese guitarist and Spring & Autumn front man Yang Meng, but with deep blues roots as well. In 2008, he cut his own album, featuring his own original songs sung in Chinese, songs that focus on the daily lives of working-class people in China. That year, I saw a concert of Zhou Chao playing acoustic folk guitar at Yuyintang, taking the crowd on a mystical spirit-journey deep into Central Asia with his tunes, which were raga-like instrumental performances full of his original improvisations.

Shanghai punk band Banana Monkey with lead singer Bono performing at Yuyintang on 9 July 2016 (photo by Andrew Field)

Yuyintang also featured regular performances by Alec Haavik, an accomplished jazz saxophonist and wind instrumentalist, who has played a significant role in shaping and driving Shanghai's jazz scene since his arrival in 2005. It seems that no live music venue in Shanghai could subsist on rock alone, and most of the longstanding ones like Yuyintang offered up an eclectic range of performers, musical genres, and styles.

Yet rock was the favored music at Yuyingtang. On 9 July 2016, I attended a show there, which reinforced the eclecticism of this rock club scene, but also highlighted the strong and continuous Beijing influence over Shanghai's rock scene. The event was organized by a young American hipster, music expert, and self-proclaimed hustler named Brian Offenther, who had been working for several years in Shanghai and elsewhere in Asia as a journalist, DJ, and music event organizer. The concert featured four bands. The headliner band Hang on the Box was a veteran punk band from Beijing that claimed to be the first all-female punk band in China. The band, which came together after many years for a reunion, was fronted by female singer Wang Yue. She started her career as a punk singer in Beijing's Scream Bar in 1998 with a screaming performance of her own. At Yuyintang, they offered up a set of rather slow-paced but intense songs with a strong feminist message behind them. The other bands including a metal band called Goushen, the all-foreigner Shanghai-based punk band Round Eye, and another veteran of the Chinese garage scene in Shanghai, Banana Monkey, who I'd first seen perform at the Rock It Festival in 2007. They ended up stealing the show with a highly energetic performance led by their front man, Bono. This eclectic lineup was reminiscent of the concerts and festivals staged by Liu Miao and Gao Feng, the owners of the Beijing club 2 Kolegas.

As if in testament to this connection between the two clubs,

I would finally get a chance to renew my acquaintance with Liu Miao at Yuyintang many years after I had last seen him at 2 Kolegas. In the interim, Liu Miao joined with a musician named Zhang Wei and his brother Mickey Zhang, a DJ, as well as female bassist Yu Qiao, to form an experimental rock band called WHAI. The band started out at 2 Kolegas in October 2012 and developed a following over the next few years. On the night of 5 January 2018, I headed to Yuyintang to see the much-touted band perform. With Liu Miao keeping a strong, steady beat on the drums, Zhang Wei singing and playing electric guitar, and Yu Qiao on bass, and the other Zhang performing on a keyboard, the band played a drum-and-bass heavy set of experimental, 'psychedelic' tunes also with a heavy dose of electronica. This band was another indicator of a trend that I witnessed in Beijing and which other followers of the scene acknowledged, that indie rock bands in Beijing were experimenting more and more with fusions of electronic, dancehall, and other styles of music.

The Brief Life of Windows Tembo and Windows Underground
Windows was a club chain in Shanghai run by African migrants to China that mainly featured hip-hop or house music for a hard-drinking and dancing crowd of Chinese and foreigners, who came for the music and the cheap drinks. In 2008, the club chain branched out into rock music as well. The first Windows club to feature rock bands was called Windows Tembo, which opened in spring 2008. I caught a SUBS concert there that April, and although the band was as good as ever, the venue itself was clearly not well-designed for the needs of a punk rock music scene. While I appreciated the chance to renew my connection with SUBS band members after several months of being away from Beijing, this was the only time I would visit Windows Tembo. Caught in the narrow space of the club, jam-packed with

A tightly packed crowd watches SUBS perform at the short-lived Windows Tembo in Shanghai in 2008 (photo by Andrew Field)

drunken, moshing people, for some reason I nearly ended up in a fistfight with an unidentified stranger with SUBS music blasting all around us before coming to my senses and exiting the club for a breather. The incident was a personal reminder of how much the design of club spaces can influence the clubbing experience for better or worse.

Soon after that, the venue stopped hosting live bands. Then in June, another venue called Windows Underground opened on the famous thoroughfare, Nanjing West Road. I paid several visits to this club over the next few months, which became quite popular among the rock afficionados of Shanghai. One night saw the veteran Beijing rock band Second-Hand Rose (二手玫瑰), a band that had formed in 2000. Their lead singer Liang Long was famous for his tendency to cross-dress in the style of old Peking opera.

Over the previous year of frequenting the indie rock scene

in Shanghai and Beijing, I often ran into fellow American 'Handlebar' Dan Shapiro who also he fronted his own band, Rogue Transmission. This was one of many rock bands in Shanghai that were composed of foreigners rather than Chinese. The following week, I headed back to Windows Underground to catch Dan and his band play their progressive, hard-driving rock. In the process, I also became reacquainted with the Beijing punk band Joyside and their own front man, Bian Yuan. After Rogue Transmission finished their set, Joyside performed a set that included their cover of the Lords of the New Church song 'Russian Roulette'. Windows Underground was on the way to becoming the premier venue for hosting Beijing bands in Shanghai, that is, until the new Mao Livehouse opened.

Shanghai's Very Own Mao Livehouse

The following year, the Beijing outfit that ran MAO Live House opened a club in Shanghai. The venue was first located in Red Town (红坊), a factory warehouse-turned-art district at the western end of Huaihai Road that bore some comparison to Beijing's 798 Art Zone. It opened in September 2009 out of an old dance club called Candy, with a capacity of 800 guests, more than any other rock venue in town size-wise except the Zhijiang Dream Factory. The club was the product of a partnership between the Japanese label, Bad News Records, which opened the original MAO Livehouse in Beijing in 2007, and the Shanghai-based label Soma Records. Its director was Li Dalong, the lead singer of the Shanghai rock band Crystal Butterfly. I attended a few shows there, including one in January 2010 hosted by Maybe Mars and featuring Beijing indie rock bands P.K. 14, the Gar, 24 Hours, and Rustic. During that concert, I caught up briefly with Michael Pettis and Yang Haisong, both in attendance at the concert which was showcasing their label. The event filled the entire house with music enthusiasts, showing once again the power of Beijing rock bands to attract a big crowd in Shanghai.

In early 2011, after a 16-month stint in that location, the club changed venues to an office building on the corner of Chongqing South Road and Jianguo Road. This was near the Tianzifang 田子坊tourist area on Taikang Road, and not far from where the club 4 Live once stood. Tianzifang is Shanghai's version of Nanluoguxiang in Beijing, a working-class neighborhood of old unused factory spaces and lively lane-house residences that in the early 2000s were occupied by dozens of art studios and galleries, then by shops, restaurants, cafes, and bars. The symmetry between the MAO Livehouses in Beijing and Shanghai was apparent in their locations near thriving commercial sites made up of old historic buildings and residential neighborhoods transformed for tourism. I was there for the opening night of the new Mao Livehouse on 308 Chongqing South Road, on the third floor of the building that also housed Shanghai's famous Yue Opera troupe.

The band performing on the club's opening night was the Yunnanese band Mountain Men. The band played a combination of modern and traditional Chinese instruments, and the music was a blend of good old rock'n'roll or reggae-like tunes along with traditional Chinese 'mountain songs' and parodies of revolutionary music from the Mao years. The whole band joined in the chorus backing up the lead singer. They also sang and danced on stage in unison, as if they were performing a tribal ritual or else mimicking a 1960s American R&B band. The large audience of mostly Chinese young people was tame and subdued at first, but over time they warmed up and started to dance, goaded on by the lead singer.

Over the next few years, Mao Livehouse was the premier rock club in town, hosting big events featuring big-name bands from

Beijing and abroad. SUBS, who performed there in 2011, was just one of many Beijing-based rock bands hosted by the club. Like Yuyintang, it also hosted other events and other styles of music to fill the gap. Whereas Beijing's MAO Livehouse could pretty much fill up the club every night with rock bands and their fans, Shanghai's Mao Livehouse struggled to attract a steady crowd with a much greater variety of performance styles and other special events. Even so, the club's development was unsteady, and it closed many times over the next several years, partly due to low attendance and partly for licensing reasons. Yet as of 2022, it had survived in its present location and still booked a variety of rock bands from Beijing and elsewhere in China, at least when the city or parts of it weren't being locked down in the new age of COVID.

Between the 2000s and 2010s, Shanghai's bid to build a sustained network of clubs dedicated to rock music faced many challenges. In a city in which young people were encouraged to take up classical piano, in which there are only two or three shops dedicated to rock guitarists as opposed to dozens of piano shops, in which nighttime fun usually amounted to sitting in a lounge in a crowded disco or belting out Cantonese songs in a KTV house, in which residential compounds are so tightly clustered that rock venues have trouble even existing, in which the foreign population swelled to hundreds of thousands, only to diminish in the wake of localization, pollution, and other factors, not to mention the onset of the global COVID pandemic in 2020, it is amazing that Shanghai was able to sustain a rock scene of its own. Yet as of 2021, rock clubs in the city were more powerful and numerous than ever. And Shanghai's rock scene was possibly even more dynamic than the scene in Beijing, once the undisputed rock capital of China.

Meanwhile, many other cities in China have developed rock

scenes and clubs of their own. This was true not just for Wuhan, but also for other provincial capital cities such as Xi'an, Chengdu, Changsha, Hangzhou, and Nanjing. Even Suzhou, a smaller city just to the west of Shanghai, had a rock club scene featuring original bands. Guangzhou had always had a relatively large music scene, and out in Yunnan, Kunming has had featured rock bars since at least the early 2000s. As Beijing's star fell, and the capital city lost its status as China's sole rock mecca, other cities picked up the slack, developed their own rock bands, clubs, and festivals, and continued to carry the rock and roll banner into the future. Among these cities, Shanghai, with its relatively sizable international community and cosmopolitan outlook, remained at the forefront, but even so, other cities such as Chengdu developed their own distinctive music scenes out of amalgamations of rock, hip-hop, electronic music and other sounds and scenes. Metal music continued to grind on, and Shanghai and other cities had their own metal scenes as well.

By the 2020s, as I was wrapping up this book, two opposing forces shaped and influenced the rock scenes of China in contradictory ways. First was the rise of the COVID pandemic, which halted or at least deterred the development of music scenes in China and all over the world. Second was the increasing popularity of Chinese social media sites and programs that elevated the indie rock bands of Beijing and elsewhere in China to new heights of national stardom.

Epilogue

Rock Scenes in China in the Wake of the Global Pandemic

The viral pandemic known as COVID-19 erupted in China around the beginning of 2020 and quickly made its way around the world, shutting down all sorts of public activities in the process, including live music scenes. In February, I left China for a spell to go back to the United States, for a total of seven months. I returned to China in September 2020, to find it — well, sort of normal. Over the previous few months, employing a combination of heavy-handed policies, including shutdowns, the government in China had succeeded in quelling the spread of the pandemic, which had started in the SUBS's hometown of Wuhan. For several months, people all over China hunkered down in their homes with very limited mobility. Yet by the summer of 2020, life was returning to normal and business establishments, including live music venues, were re-opening. To be sure, there were still many restrictions and cautions in place, people wore masks in public spaces, and the government tested and traced people frequently. But for the most part, life was inching back to normal in China as the rest of the world suffered catastrophic losses and the complete disruption of live music, which during the pandemic meant watching a performer's show on your laptop computer screen as it streamed live via the internet.

ROCKING THE CHINESE NATION

Among foreigners living in China, those who had bided their time in their apartments and homes could now re-emerge into the public spaces and once again enjoy the lifestyles of cities like Shanghai and Beijing. Meanwhile, those who had left China at the onset of the pandemic were finding it difficult to return. I was one of the lucky ones, since I had a work visa and received a special invitation from my university to return. Others were not so lucky, and many thousands of foreign students, workers, teachers, and musicians waited a long time to return to China, while many others gave up on China and re-settled in their own home countries.

Not long after emerging from the then mandatory two-week quarantine period, I could step out into the streets of Shanghai and visit local restaurants, bars, and clubs. This was also true of the city of Kunshan, where I spend most of my time now, and in the neighboring city of Suzhou. Later that fall, I traveled to Suzhou with my filmmaking partner Jud Willmont (co-director of our film on Chinese indie rock) to visit the Wave Live Bar, where we caught a live performance by the Carsick Cars. Now they are a veteran Chinese rock band and a well-known name in China and abroad. That night they put on a marvelous show to a tightly packed venue with hundreds of young people, mostly Chinese, writhing and shaking to their rhythms and singing along to all their songs.

One of the reasons why Carsick Cars was so popular now is that they were featured on an online TV show called "Summer of the Bands" (乐队的夏天). This Chinese production, sponsored by the Modern Sky label, took indie rock in China to new heights, introducing the bands to an audience of millions. Young people who had never had a chance to be exposed to the gritty rock club scenes of Beijing or Shanghai, or even the music festivals, could now watch these bands compete for the top spot in the show. In addition to Carsick Cars, Joyside also enjoyed a revival through this show, as did Hedgehog and other bands that I'd seen in tiny 2 Kolegas thirteen years before. The success of the show gave new life to China's indie rock scene and packed countless thousands of young people into the gritty live clubs in cities all over China.

Later that fall, Jud and I went to see our favorite band, SUBS, who were performing at the Modern Sky Lab in Shanghai. After undergoing many different permutations, while keeping the band alive, Kang Mao and Wu Hao were still rocking strong, this time with a new drummer. Kang Mao gave a riveting performance that night, including a song that involved her placing a white veil over her face. Her theatrics and energetic performance style had not diminished one iota since I first saw her in 2 Kolegas in 2007. Neither had Wu Hao's rock guitar skills. The entire crowd of hundreds, again mostly Chinese, was swaying and slamming to the shouts, chants and cries of Kang Mao and SUBS. Chinese indie rock was alive and well in Shanghai and Suzhou and thriving in nearly every corner of China. The main difference was that now the audience was mainly Chinese, not foreigners. The role of foreigners as supporters, initiators, sparks, agents, guides, and fans had declined over the years. Now in the haze of the pandemic era, and with China virtually closed off to the outside world, it was the turn of the Chinese to take the main stage and make rock music their very own.

While Beijing's role as China's rock epicenter had greatly diminished since I first documented the indie rock scene in that golden year of 2007, rock music scenes had emerged and flourished in cities all over China. As of 2021, one could attend dedicated rock clubs and music festivals in just about every major city and watch local homegrown rock bands perform. No longer did these bands have to make the long journey to Beijing to prove themselves. The wildly popular show Summer of the

ROCKING THE CHINESE NATION

Bands not only revived the careers of old Beijing bands like Joyside and Hedgehog, but it also spurred a new generation of Chinese youths to grab guitars and mics and make their own original music. At the same time, the power of social media was exposing Chinese youths to more styles and sounds of music from all over the world. The youths of China in 2022 are far savvier than those of fifteen years ago, when indie rock scenes in China were largely an underground urban phenomenon.

In the spring of 2022, another phase of the pandemic walloped Shanghai as the Omicron version of the virus spread rapidly through the urban population, compelling the city government to shut down the city entirely for around two months between April and May and confining 25 million people to their homes. While I waited out the lockdown, I wondered what effect this would have on Shanghai and its live music scenes. Meanwhile, Beijing experienced a shorter and less uniform wave of lockdowns. As summer came around, both cities opened once again as life returned to normal, or at least a semblance thereof.

With the end of stringent COVID controls in late 2022, 2023 saw the rekindling of live scenes all over China. New hope has emerged that rock music will once again have space to grow, develop and flourish in Shanghai, Beijing, and other Chinese cities. With the fertile ground prepared by Chinese rock veterans like Cui Jian — who in April 2022 staged a live concert broadcast on the social media platform WeChat viewed by millions — and the seeds planted by Michael Pettis, Yang Haisong, and so many others — indie rock and other forms of independent music may indeed have a bright future in China. And perhaps someday some of these bands will be household names around the world.

A Selected Bibliography

Baranovich, Nimrod, *China's New Voices: Popular Music, Ethnicity, Gender, and Politics, 1978-1997* (Berkeley, 2003)

Campbell, Jonathan, *Red Rock: The Long, Strange March of Chinese Rock & Roll* (Hong Kong, 2011)

De Kloet, Jeroen, *China with a Cut: Globalization, Urban Youth, and Popular Music* (Amsterdam, 2010)

Farrer, James and Andrew David Field, *Shanghai Nightscapes: A Nocturnal Biography of a Global Metropolis* (Chicago, 2015)

Field, Andrew David, *Shanghai's Dancing World: Cabaret Culture and Urban Politics, 1919-1954* (Hong Kong, 2010)

Field, Andrew David, and Jeroen Groenewegen, 'Explosive Acts: Beijing's Punk Rock Scene in the Postmodern World of 2007' in *Berliner China Hefte*, Vol. 34 (2008): 8-26.

Field, Andrew David, '"Beijing is Rock, Shanghai is Jazz: Musical Identity Formations and Shifts in the Big City Soundscapes of China" in Brett Lashua and Stephen Wagg, eds., *Sounds and The City, Volume 2* (Palgrave Macmillan, 2018) 151-172.

Gendron, Bernard, *From Montmartre to the Mudd Club: Popular Music and the Avant-Garde* (Chicago, 2002)

Groenwegen, Jeroen, *The Performance of Identity in Chinese Popular Music* (dissertation, Leiden, 2011)

Johnson, Ian, *The Souls of China: The Return of Religion After Mao* (New York, 2017)

Jones, Andrew F., *Like a Knife: Ideology and Genre in Contemporary Chinese Popular Music* (Ithaca, 1992)

O'Dell, David, *Inseparable: The Memoirs of an American and the*

Story of Chinese Punk Rock (lulu.com, 2014)

Peterson, Richard and Andy Bennett, eds., *Music Scenes: Local, Translocal, and Virtual* (Nashville, TN, 2011)

Wasserstrom, Jeffrey, and Elizabeth Perry, eds., *Popular Protest and Political Culture in Modern China, Second Edition* (Boulder, CO, 1994).

Wu Hung, *Remaking Beijing* (Chicago, 2005)

About The Author

Andrew Field is the author of many books and articles on the history of nightlife, dance, and music in urban China. He has produced independent documentary films on jazz and rock music scenes in China. He lives in Shanghai and in the neighboring city of Kunshan, where he serves as Associate Professor of Chinese History at Duke Kunshan University.

www.ingramcontent.com/pod-product-compliance
Lightning Source LLC
LaVergne TN
LVHW031611060526
838201LV00065B/4813